||| || | ||||||||| | ||| ||| || ||||||||||| | | |||
W9-CZK-409

☀ INSIGHT **COMPACT GUIDE**

IRELAND

Compact Guide: Ireland is the ultimate quick-reference guide to this fascinating destination. It tells you all you'll ever need to know about the attractions of both the Republic of Ireland and Northern Ireland, from the sophistication of Dublin to the bleak grandeur of the Gaeltacht, from the breathtaking beauty of Killarney to the astonishing geometry of the Giant's Causeway.

This is one of more than 133 Compact Guides, which combine the interests and enthusiasms of two of the world's best known information providers: Insight Guides, whose titles have set the standard for visual travel guides since 1970, and Discovery Channel, the world's premier source of nonfiction television programming.

APA PUBLICATIONS
Part of the Langenscheidt Publishing Group

Insight Compact Guide: Ireland

Written by: Bernd Müller
Updated by: Rachel Warren
Photography: Richard Nowitz, Geray Sweeney, Marcus Wilson-Smith
Additional photography: Pete Bennett 69, 70/2, 71, 79/2; Berlitz 43/2, 65/1; Collections/Michael Diggin 93/2; Collections/Image Ireland/Bob Brien 92; Collections/Image Ireland/Alain Le Garsmeur 94, 95/1, 95/2; Alamy/Andre Jenny 78; Alamy/Brian Harris 18/19; Corbis/Geray Sweeney 93; Jason Mitchell 39/1, 57
Cover photograph: Aldo Torelli/Getty Images
Maps: Polyglott/Buchhaupt

Editorial Director: Brian Bell
Managing Editor: Maria Lord

CONTACTING THE EDITORS: As every effort is made to provide accurate information in this publication, we would appreciate it if readers would call our attention to any errors and omissions by contacting:
Apa Publications, PO Box 7910, London SE1 1WE, England.
Fax: (44 20) 7403 0290
e-mail: insight@apaguide.co.uk

Information has been obtained from sources believed to be reliable, but its accuracy and completeness, and the opinions based thereon, are not guaranteed.

© 2005 APA Publications GmbH & Co. Verlag KG Singapore Branch, Singapore.

First Edition 1996. Second Edition 2002, updated 2005, reprinted 2005
Printed in Singapore by Insight Print Services (Pte) Ltd
Original edition © Polyglott-Verlag Dr Bolte KG, Munich

Distributed in the UK & Ireland by:
GeoCenter International Ltd
The Viables Centre, Harrow Way, Basingstoke,
Hampshire RG22 4BJ
Tel: (44 1256) 817987, Fax: (44 1256) 817988

Distributed in the United States by:
Langenscheidt Publishers, Inc.
36–36 33rd Street 4th Floor, Long Island City, New York 11106
Tel: (1 718) 784-0055, Fax: (1 718) 784-0640

Worldwide distribution enquiries:
APA Publications GmbH & Co. Verlag KG (Singapore Branch)
38 Joo Koon Road, Singapore 628990
Tel: (65) 6865-1600, Fax: (65) 6861-6438

www.insightguides.com

Introduction

Places

Culture

Practical Information

◁ **Glendalough (p42)**
This secluded Wicklow valley with its round tower and monastic ruins can evoke a deep longing for peace and solitude.

▷ **Dublin (p20–30)**
Trinity College's Long Room Library recalls the city's tradition of learning, but Dublin's compact size, its mixture of tradition and modernity and its great talent for having fun have made it a top holiday destination.

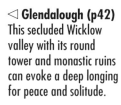

▽ **Aran Islands (p73)**
Straddling the mouth of Galway Bay, these islands keep alive old traditions.

△ **Newgrange (p35)**
Some remarkable burial mounds and passage graves in the Boyne Valley make this one of Europe's richest prehistoric sites.

◁ **Cork (p54–7)**
This south-coast port has a gentle charm and a people known for their rapid-fire conversation.

△ **Giant's Causeway (p97)** On the northwest coast lies this strange formation of 40,000 hexagonal basalt columns.

◁ **The Burren (p70)** This deeply fissured and barren limestone plateau in north Clare, with its delicate flora, is a place of pilgrimage for botanists and geologists.

▽ **Belfast (p100–5)** Its botanical gardens are less well-known than its sectarian divisions, but Ireland's only industrial city is a vibrant place.

▷ **Dingle Peninsula (p65)** The area's beauty and fierce storms were captured in David Lean's movie *Ryan's Daughter.*

◁ **Galway (p71–3)** This bustling university town has a strong arts scene and a love of festivals and horse racing.

Ireland – Mystery and Mischievousness

Opposite: the green, green grass of Kinsale

An extraterrestrial statistician visiting Ireland would have a hard time accounting for its enduring appeal to holidaymakers. The rainfall is high, as is the cost of living. Terrorism has chalked up a daunting death toll, in one part of the island at least. There are no massive theme parks. The sea is cold. Yet people really do fall in love with the place, just like the brochures say, and keep coming back. It all seems very mysterious.

But then mystery lies at the heart of the Irish character, surfacing in all manner of ways, from the sacred mysteries of the influential Roman Catholic religion to the magical ways of the little people, the mischievous leprechauns who weave their way through Celtic folklore. It is this Celtic inheritance that sets Ireland apart, in the same way as it makes Brittany distinct from the rest of France. Although English is universally spoken, the ghost of the old Gaelic language is lurking close to its surface, conferring even on everyday conversation the elliptical quality of an incomplete jigsaw puzzle. The people have a strong sense of theatricality. This is best expressed in their reckless conviviality and whimsical view of life, though it can all too abruptly veer into wistfulness, self-absorption and melancholy.

Below: Tara brooch, from the National Museum of Ireland
Bottom: the Viking heritage is still remembered in Dublin

For the visitor, this ethereal atmosphere, this 18th-century pace of life that has not completely faded away, becomes an alluring cocktail when mixed with the celebrated surfeit of ravishing scenery. It's only when you sober up and try to understand the place that the difficulties set in.

THE PAST, PROPAGANDA AND PEACE

Central to this understanding is history. Ireland has history the way the Sahara has sand. The past suffuses the present so thoroughly that people refer casually to the events of bygone centuries as though they had taken place yesterday. The past matters here, in a way it does in few other Western nations. Largely, this is because of Ireland's

Below: an emigration statue in Co. Cork remembers the families who left for America

Bottom: today's Ireland has one of Europe's youngest populations

fraught relationship with England. Over the centuries, England subjugated Ireland for strategic reasons, exploited it and, worst of all, ignored it. In the end, not really knowing how to cope with its intractable neighbour, it divided it.

The consequences of that division in 1921 have kept Ireland in the world headlines over the past 30 years. The conflicting secular loyalties in Northern Ireland of a million Protestants, who wanted to remain part of Britain, and more than half a million Roman Catholics, who felt a closer bond with the Republic of Ireland, erupted into violence in 1969 and spawned a vicious terrorism. Widely portrayed as a religious conflict, it had more to do with an insecure national identity and with a realisation that, in an economically depressed area with too few jobs and houses to go round, each tribe had to fight for its fair share.

However strident the propaganda from each side, behind the scenes the tourist authorities of both parts of Ireland co-operated in cross-border schemes such as developing and promoting inland waterway links. And, when a ceasefire was declared in 1994, it wasn't long before entrepreneurs began offering adventurous visitors bus tours of Belfast's most illustrious battlegrounds.

The intensification of peace efforts has given rise to renewed optimism in the North, which it is hoped will benefit tourism. Certainly, visitors

can profitably explore the differing delights of both North and South, as we do in this book. Regardless of where you go, you are guaranteed one of the world's greatest welcomes.

POSITION AND SIZE

Ireland is an island in the Atlantic to the west of Great Britain. Its northernmost point, Malin Head in Donegal, lies on the same latitude as Ayr in southern Scotland and Odense in Denmark, and its southernmost point, Mizen Head in County Cork, is on a level with London and Dortmund.

To understand Ireland's geology it's best to think of it in cross-section as a bowl: the interior is mostly a limestone basin, and the only real mountains are around the rim. To the northwest and along the east coast this rim is made of granite, in the south and southwest of sandstone, and in the northeast of basalt (including the famous Giant's Causeway rock formation). Ireland gets its name 'the emerald isle' from the fertile central basin, with its lakes and lush green fields.

The four provinces of Ireland – Leinster in the east, Munster in the south, Connaught in the west and Ulster in the north – are named after the country's former kingdoms. Although these regions have no administrative significance today, Ireland's political geography cannot be adequately described without them. Of the 32 counties on the island, 26 belong to the Republic and six (of the nine that form the province of Ulster) to Northern Ireland. 'Northern' doesn't quite reflect geographical reality: the northernmost point of Ireland lies in the Republic.

Vital Statistics

The total population of the island is approximately 6 million (4.5 million in Eire and 1.5 million in Northern Ireland). The total surface area of the whole island is 84,500sq km (32,600sq miles), with the Republic of Ireland taking up 70,300sq km (27,100sq miles) and Northern Ireland another 14,180sq km (5,470sq miles). The longest river is the Shannon (386km/ 239 miles), and the largest lake is Lough Neagh in Northern Ireland (29km/18 miles long and 17km/10 miles wide, making it the biggest in the British Isles). The tallest mountain to be found in the Republic of Ireland is Carrantuohill (1,041m/ 3,410ft) in Macgillicuddy's Reeks, Kerry, and the tallest in Northern Ireland is Slieve Donard (850m/ 2,790ft) in the Mountains of Mourne, County Down.

CLIMATE AND WHEN TO GO

Ireland has a moderate Atlantic climate, influenced by the Gulf Stream. The seasons do not change dramatically – the average annual temperature is around 10°C (50°F). The coldest months in the year are January and February with daily averages of between 5°C (41°F) and 8°C (46°F), and

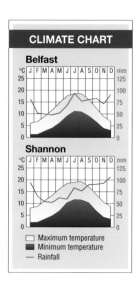

CLIMATE CHART

Belfast

Shannon

☐ Maximum temperature
■ Minimum temperature
— Rainfall

the weather is at its warmest during August, when it reaches an average of 16°C (60°F). The southeastern part of the country has the greatest number of sunny days in the year, the southwest has the mildest winters and the northeast gets the most frost.

The Irish are often quite proud of their rain statistics, recalling the 23 rainy days in August 1986 or the 309 rainy days experienced by Ballinahinch in Galway in the year 1923. In contrast, everyone looks forward to a 'grand soft day', when the drizzle seems warm and pleasant and doesn't really feel wet at all. The east has the lowest precipitation, and the wettest place on the island is the mountainous southwest. Whatever the season, there's one golden rule: be prepared for sudden changes in the weather.

The most popular time for visits to Ireland is between May and October. The sunniest months are May and June, and in recent years temperatures have been unusually high, sometimes reaching 30°C (86°F). Ireland is by no means empty when the rest of Europe is on holiday, and such tourist attractions as the Giant's Causeway or the Ring of Kerry are often overcrowded in peak season. Those who are not tied to midsummer holidays prefer to travel to Ireland in May or in early autumn, when the island is usually a lot more idyllic.

A tourist draw all year round: Dublin's Georgian heritage

FLORA AND FAUNA

The oak forests that covered the island in pre-historic times have largely disappeared, apart from a few strictly protected remnants, and most of the re-afforestation of recent years has been limited to fast-growing commercial timber. Grazing land separated by hedges is a typical feature of the Irish landscape, and so is moorland.

High moors with heather and fern alternate with peat bogs, which are formed whenever the moss, known as *sphagnum*, starts to spread in low-lying, poorly-irrigated regions. Commercial peat-cutting has been destroying a lot of these regions, however, and steps are being taken to ensure the survival of Ireland's bogs and moors.

Animal life does feature the odd peculiarity: the Irish hare, for instance, which unlike its European cousin is more closely related to the Arctic variety, and also a species of bat which is very rarely found anywhere else in Europe. Wild goats live in the more remote mountain regions, and Connemara has its famous wild ponies. Common English animals such as the weasel and the mole do not exist in Ireland, and the absence of snakes is traditionally attributed to their banishment by St Patrick *(see page78)*. As for marine life, there are probably more dolphins off the south and west coast of Ireland than anywhere else in Europe.

THE PEOPLE

Calling the Irish Celts is like saying all French are Normans – the Celts who settled in Ireland were followed by Vikings, Normans, Scottish and English, to name but a few. The most important part of the Celtic heritage for the Irish is their Gaelic language, which was replaced by English as the national tongue during the 19th century and has been systematically re-promoted only since the foundation of the Irish Free State in 1922. Today, Gaelic is taught in all schools in the Republic (though it has been taken off the compulsory list) and is the country's official language. Surveys show that around 32 percent of the population in the Republic and more than 5 percent in North-

Where There's Smoke
The characteristic smell of peat fires pervades much of Ireland's countryside. Since the 17th century the bogs have been exploited as an inexpensive source of fuel. During the famine (1845–51) dried peat was often the only fuel available. In recent times, more efficient methods of cutting the peat have put an extra strain on Irish bogs and, although peat fires smell lovely in winter, the remaining bogs are to be protected from commercial exploitation.

The tradition of learning continues at the National Library in Dublin

ern Ireland can speak Gaelic fluently. It is a first language for only 1 to 2 percent of the Irish as a whole; they live in the regions known collectively as *Gaeltacht*, mostly in the west along coastal strips in Galway and Mayo and also in Donegal.

Below: music is an important part of the Gaelic tradition
Bottom: watching over Healy Pass, in the southwest

RELIGION

Roman Catholicism in the Republic of Ireland is not constitutional, but a *de facto* state religion. According to the most recent census, 91.6 percent of the population are Catholics, and 82 percent of those said they attended mass regularly. The figure was 95 percent a decade ago, so attendance is falling, but nevertheless the percentage is higher than that of any other European country, including Poland. Although the church's influence is still strong in education and daily life, recent controversies about birth control and divorce are another sign that the hold of the church is significantly waning, especially in the Dublin area.

The six counties of Northern Ireland are dominated by the strict form of Protestantism known as Presbyterianism. Although only 21.4 percent of the population describe themselves as Presbyterians, almost 50 percent said they were Protestant believers (including members of the Church of Ireland and Methodists). Just under 40 percent describe themselves as Catholics.

THE ECONOMY

Agriculture (primarily cattle breeding, dairy farming, and potato and maize cultivation) has been the traditional mainstay of the Irish economy for many centuries and still is today, though industrial production (brewing, food processing, textiles, chemicals and electronics) now contributes most to the country's GNP.

Both sectors profited from Ireland's European Union membership as far as investment and price stability were concerned, and the economic outlook improved dramatically during the 1980s and 1990s, with a marked decrease in unemployment and some forecasts even suggesting that the Republic would soon have a higher per capita income than Britain.

But many of the remarkable concessions Ireland had managed to extract from the European Union – generous tax holidays and building grants for incoming industries, for example – began to expire, and the 'Celtic tiger' economy became less insulated from febrile world trading conditions. In particular, the Republic's adoption of the euro in 2002 restricted its ability to protect itself by varying its interest and currency rates.

The UK remains one of the Republic's largest trading partners, accounting for some 20 percent of its exports. Tourism is by far the most important part of the service sector, with about 4 million people a year visiting the Republic.

The region around Belfast has been the industrial centre of Ireland since the 19th century, and Northern Ireland still has a lingering legacy of shipbuilding, aviation and textiles. Industrial investment in Northern Ireland has been largely subsidised by the British government, but developments such as EU membership, weak unions and low wages have attracted American and Asian firms. Both parts of Ireland have often competed with attractive subsidies to lure the same foreign investors to their own side of the border.

In common with Britain, Northern Ireland did not adopt the euro in 2002. Price differentials between the two parts of the country encourage a great deal of cross-border shopping.

Gaelic Phrases

Dia duit May God bless you
Dia is Muire duit May God and Mary bless you. (Reply)
Conas atá tu? How are you?
Sláinte Cheers
Slán Bye
Scileann fíon fírinne Wine lets out the truth
Saol fada chugot Long life to you
Sláinte chugat Good health to you
Is fear rith maith ná drochsheasamh A good run is better than a bad stand
Go n-ithe an cat thú is go n-ithe an diabol an cat May the cat eat you, and may the cat be eaten by the devil
Go néirí bothair leat May the road rise to meet you

Fashion on display in Molesworth Street, Dublin

POLITICS AND ADMINISTRATION

The 26 counties that formed the Irish Free State in 1922 now constitute the Republic of Ireland. In 1998, as part of the peace initiative in the North, the Republic abandoned the territorial claim in its 1937 constitution to the six counties of Northern Ireland which remain under British rule, and it accepted that any eventual unification of the island would depend on the consent of the majority of voters in Northern Ireland.

GOVERNMENT

The Republic's head of state is a directly elected president. This was a largely ceremonial position until Mary Robinson became the first woman president in 1990; a liberal-minded lawyer, she vigorously supported women's causes and helped to create a new sense of confidence in the Republic. Her term of office set the tone for her successor, Mary McAleese *(see box, right),* in 1997.

The House of Representatives *(Dáil)* has 166 members *(Teachtaí Dála,* usually abbreviated to TD), and is directly elected every five years. The largest parties are the conservative *Fianna Fáil* ('soldiers of destiny') and the marginally less conservative *Fine Gael* ('family of Gaels'). The second house of parliament, the Senate *(Seanad Éireann),* consists of 11 members directly

Visual communication: murals (below) are Belfast's message boards, and (bottom) Ireland's convivial side is represented by pubs

appointed by the prime minister and 49 who are indirectly elected. The head of government is known as the *Taoiseach* (Gaelic for 'chieftain').

Northern Ireland is part of the United Kingdom of Great Britain and Northern Ireland (i.e. *not* part of 'Great Britain'). It is often known as 'Ulster' – though that term more precisely applies to the nine counties of the ancient Irish province of Ulster. For 70 years it was governed by its own parliament in Belfast, regarded by many of the Unionists who dominated it as 'a Protestant parliament for a Protestant people'. Since Ulster has a sizeable Catholic minority, this system led to civil disturbances which made Northern Ireland virtually ungovernable, and resulted in the body being dissolved in 1972: for most of the next three decades, the province was ruled directly from London.

THE NORTHERN IRELAND DEBATE

After prolonged peace talks, a Northern Ireland Assembly was created in 1998, bringing sworn enemies from both Unionist ('loyalists', almost exclusively Protestant) and Republican (nationalists, predominantly Catholic) parties around the same table. Unionists, however, refused to play a significant role until Republican terrorists began handing over their weapons.

At the end of 1999, the British government devolved certain powers to the Assembly and to a new power-sharing executive; the British and Irish governments signed the British-Irish agreement; and the IRA appointed a representative to liaise with an independent commission on the decommissioning of weapons. Ironies abounded: for example, Martin McGuinness, a former IRA leader and now a Sinn Féin politician, became minister of education, responsible for the schooling of both Protestant and Catholic children.

Assembly debates were sometimes conciliatory but more often fractious, and sectarian killing and intimidation continued at a reduced level, much of it in Belfast's ghettos. Hope and despair, familiar partners in Irish affairs, continue to keep the outcome uncertain.

Presidential election
Mary McAleese secceeded Mary Robinson's as president of the Republic of Ireland in 1997. It is part of the Alice in Wonderland nature of Irish politics that Mary McAleese, a Belfast academic with strong nationalist sympathies, did not have a vote in the Republic's presidential election, yet she was able to stand as a candidate – and win. In 2004 she was nominated unopposed for a second 7-year term.

Mary McAleese, the Republic's second woman president in succession

HISTORICAL HIGHLIGHTS

ca 7000BC The earliest archaeological evidence of Mesolithic hunter-fisher people (flints, etc) found along the coast dates from this period.

From ca 3000BC Beginning of Neolithic period. Megalithic and portal tombs appear.

From ca 500BC Irish Iron Age begins with first migration of Celts from Britain.

ca AD300 Using the 'Ogham alphabet', a rune-like script develops in which stone-carved inscriptions in Old Irish are handed down.

431 The Pope sends Palladius as a bishop to Ireland, proving Christian communities existed before the arrival of St Patrick.

ca 432 St Patrick (Ireland's patron saint) returns to Ireland as a missionary. At the age of 16 he had been taken by force from Britain to Ireland, and later fled to France.

From ca 800 After a series of Viking raids in which monasteries are plundered, the Norsemen establish several settlements, including Dublin, which later grow into harbour towns.

976–1014 Brian Ború, crowned King of Munster in 976, proclaims himself High King of Ireland in 1002 and inflicts a decisive defeat on the Vikings near Clontarf in 1014. His murder leads to the kingdom's demise once again.

From 1169 Henry II sends Anglo-Normans to help Dermot MacMurrough in his fight for the Irish throne. They settle after conquering large areas. Feudalism is introduced; castles are built.

1366 Under the Statutes of Kilkenny, the English Crown attempts to stop its barons from assimilating, marrying Irish women, or speaking the Irish language.

From 1541 Henry VIII of England crowns himself King of Ireland and begins asserting British supremacy over Irish clan princes.

1607 The 'Flight of the Earls'. The most powerful of the Irish clan princes flee to France, marking the end of Gaelic supremacy in Ireland.

1608 'Ulster Plantation'. James I systematically settles Protestant Scots and English.

1641–53 Rebellion by Irish Catholics against the English settlement policy is thwarted in 1649 when Oliver Cromwell lands in Ireland and begins a campaign of brutal annihilation.

1688–91 James II, Catholic king of England, defends his throne on Irish soil against William of Orange. His defeat by William at the Battle of the Boyne in 1690 *(see page 34)* is still celebrated today by Protestants in Northern Ireland. The period of 'Protestant Ascendancy' begins. In 1691, the Irish-Protestant parliament in Dublin passes the 'Penal Laws' excluding Catholics from public office, depriving them of their property and their right to vote, and making it difficult for them to practise their religion.

From 1782 Protestant politician Henry Grattan calls for legislative independence for Dublin's parliament and revision of the Penal Laws.

1791 Influenced by revolutions in France and America, the 'United Irishmen' form in Belfast. Its leader, Wolfe Tone, a Protestant coach-builder's son, advocates 'the common name of Irishman, in place of the denominations of Protestant, Catholic and Dissenter'.

1800 The Act of Union makes Ireland part of the United Kingdom. The parliament in Dublin is dissolved and Ireland is forcibly represented by 100 MPs in the House of Commons.

1829 Catholic politician Daniel O'Connell ('the Liberator') forces the London parliament to emancipate Catholics.

From 1840 Nationalist movements gain strength (Irish Republican Brotherhood founded in 1858; Irish National Land League, 1879), and are accompanied by a renewed interest in Gaelic culture (Gaelic League formed in 1893).

1845–51 The Great Potato Famine. Potato blight, introduced from America, deprives more than one-third of the Irish population of their main source of nutrition. Unusually warm winters prevent the destruction of the fungus. An estimated 1 million people die of malnutrition, typhus and other diseases; a further 1 million emigrate. The English provide no assistance.

From 1880 The Land League and the Irish Home Rule Party led by Charles Stuart Parnell employ parliamentary means in their struggle for Irish autonomy and land reform. In 1886, Parliament in London rejects the first of several draft resolutions for Irish independence.

1905–08 Sinn Féin ('We Ourselves') is formed '...to make England take one hand from Ireland's throat and the other out of Ireland's pocket'.

1912–13 On 28 September 1912, 75 percent of Ulster Protestants sign a solemn pledge to stop attempts at autonomy 'by all necessary means'. In 1913 the Ulster Volunteer Force is formed to enforce the pledge.

1916 Easter Rising. On 24 April, 1,800 volunteers, led by Pádraig Pearse and James Connolly, occupy public buildings in Dublin and declare the formation of an Irish Republic. The rising is put down six days later. Britain's harsh response (Pearse, Connolly and 13 other rebels were executed in early May) backfires and many hitherto unsympathetic Irish begin to see the nationalist cause in a more positive light. The Easter Rising is regarded as marking the birth of an independent Ireland.

1918–23 In elections to the British Parliament, Sinn Féin win 73 of 105 Irish seats. An Irish parliament is formed in Dublin, with Éamon de Valera as president; the British government sends in troops. During the Anglo-Irish War of 1919–21 the Irish Republican Army gains the upper hand. In 1922 the Irish Parliament accepts the Anglo-Irish treaty for the foundation of an Irish Free State. The six counties of Northern Ireland with Protestant majorities (and a separate Parliament, established in 1920) are allowed to decide whether to join the Free State. In the South, civil war erupts between forces in favour of a Pan-Irish Republic (the 'New IRA') and the Free State, which wins.

1937 The Free State (Éire) adopts its own constitution. In 1949 it declares itself the Republic of Ireland; it leaves the British Commonwealth.

1939 Éire declares its neutrality during World War II. Germany supports the IRA.

1969–72 Mounting violence in Northern Ireland prompts the British to send in troops. The IRA, which has been fighting for a united Ireland since the 1930s, splits into two factions. The Provisional IRA intensifies its 'armed struggle'. The situation becomes volatile when 13 civilian demonstrators are shot dead by British soldiers on 'Bloody Sunday' in 1972. The parliament in Belfast is dissolved and Northern Ireland is henceforth ruled from London.

1973 The Republic of Ireland joins the European Economic Community.

1990 Mary Robinson becomes the first woman president of the Republic of Ireland.

1994 'Ceasefire' declared in Northern Ireland (ends in 1996 with an IRA bomb in London).

1998–9 In a referendum, voters support a self-governing all-party assembly in Northern Ireland. Terrorists refuse to hand over weapons.

1999 Britain devolves powers on Northern Ireland. IRA agrees to begin disarming.

2000 Northern Ireland Assembly is suspended temporarily. Peace efforts intensify.

2002 Republic adopts the euro as its currency.

2004 Mary McAleese elected unopposed for a second term as president.

Map
on page
22

*Previous pages: chips
off the old bog
Below: Parnell Monument in
O'Connell Street
Bottom: the Four Courts*

1: Dublin

It's often said that Dublin has nothing in common with the real Ireland, its lush green fields and craggy coasts. Dubliners are considered arrogant and even rather decadent by their more rural compatriots. This is strange, because the city doesn't seem at all self-important or supercilious.

Dublin has no 'skyline' of modern high-rises, no core of ancient architecture, no imperially planned thoroughfares and hardly any winding little streets; its architecture is modest and often rather self-effacing. Until the late 1980s a lot of its substance was mercilessly torn down. The City Corporation wasn't even following a grandiose plan, it was caving in to the demands of property speculators. Entire streets of the 18th-century houses for which Dublin is famous simply disappeared during the 1970s. The Corporation was also responsible for the ugly and incongruous municipal office buildings at Wood Quay.

Some attribute this architectural indifference to the fact that most of the grand buildings were associated with the colonial era, when the British ruled Ireland. But conservationists have made their voice heard in recent years and the vandalism has diminished. Most Dubliners now accept that the city's historic core is worth saving, especially if European Union funds can be attracted.

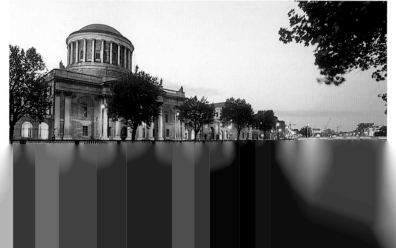

Hardly any other country in Europe is so dependent on a single metropolis. As well as being an administrative and media centre, Dublin is a magnet for artists and academics, a refuge for those trying to escape the limitations and confines of rural life, and an holiday destination for anyone interested in Irish history and culture. It's also a city where people love to communicate.

HISTORY

In 1988 Dublin concocted a 1,000th anniversary, even though there had been several settlements along the River Liffey long before 988. It was 988 that marked the incorporation of Dublin into the Kingdom of Ireland after the Norsemen were conquered by High King Mael Sechnaill. In 1170, the town was conquered by the Anglo-Normans and turned into the capital of the English-occupied region known as the 'Pale'. During the centuries that followed, Dublin was developed into the centre of Anglo-Irish administration and culture.

CAPITAL OF THE NEW REPUBLIC

During the 17th and 18th centuries Dublin thrived economically, thanks mainly to the immigration of Huguenot and Flemish weavers. At the high point of the Protestant Ascendancy, it was the second-largest city in the British Isles. After the emancipation of the Catholics in 1829, the power structure shifted: in 1841 Daniel O'Connell was voted the first Catholic mayor, and in 1851 the first Catholic university was founded (University College). In 1916 the Easter Rising began with the storming of the main post office in what is now O'Connell Street. Since 1922, Dublin has been the capital of the Irish Republic.

CITY TOUR

Anyone who wants to find their way around Dublin will need a good plan of the city: the streets tend to change their names every couple of blocks or to grow prefixes such as 'Upper' or 'Lower'. The

Below: a page from the Book of Kells *in Trinity College*
Bottom: Georgian doorway

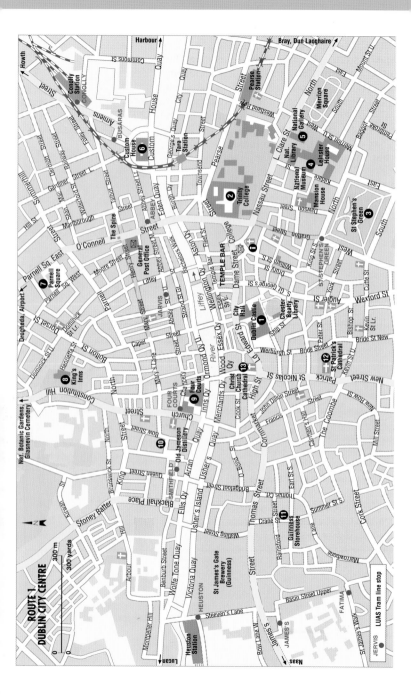

ROUTE 1
DUBLIN CITY CENTRE

numbering system is curious, too: the low house numbers run along one side of a street and the higher ones along the other. Don't despair: the city centre can easily be explored on foot, and the locals are almost always very sociable and eager to help.

The section of the centre north of the Liffey is called Dublin 1, and the southern part is Dublin 2. The region known as Dublin 4, southeast of the centre, with its well-kept Georgian houses, is a residential area favoured by intellectuals and media people; the more down-to-earth residents of the suburbs north of the river aren't all that enamoured of 'Dublin 4', and often use it adjectivally as a term of deprecation.

> Map on page 22

> **A city of many names**
> Dublin's official Gaelic name is Baile Atha Cliath (the place by the cattle ford). The Vikings called the settlement Dyfflin, from which the Old Irish Dubh Linn (black pool) is derived.

DUBLIN CASTLE

A good starting-point for exploring the city is ★ **Dublin Castle ❶** (open Mon–Fri 10am–5pm, Sun 2–5pm). Dublin Castle is essentially an elegant 18th-century palace with earlier remnants: the original Norman castle, dating from 1202, was largely ruined by fire in 1684. This site was the centre of English rule in Ireland for seven centuries and it was here, on the old main gate, that the English rulers would impale the heads of rebellious Irish chieftains.

The castle's sumptuous State Apartments, prominent among the jewels of Dublin, are open to the public. From the entrance hall a staircase leads to Battleaxe Landing, where guards armed with axes once barred the way. You then pass through a series of elegant drawing-rooms with finely decorated plasterwork ceilings (rescued from now-demolished 18th-century houses). These were formerly bedrooms used by royal visitors. In another of these rooms is an impressive Van Dyck portrait of the Countess of Southampton. The Bermingham Tower, which dates from 1411 and was rebuilt in 1775, was formerly the state prison.

As you exit on to Dame Street from the castle's upper yard, you find **City Hall**, an imposing Corinthian structure designed in 1769 as the Royal Exchange. An interesting exhibition tells *The Story of the Capital* (Mon–Sat 10am– 5.15pm). Across

Dublin Castle, formerly the centre of English power

Map on page 22

*Above: a bar in Temple Bar
Below: students at
Trinity College*

the City Hall's gardens is the **Chester Beatty Library** (Mon–Fri 10am–5pm, Sat 11am–5pm, Sun 1–5pm; Oct–Apr closed Mon), an intriguing collection of illustrated medieval manuscripts, rare books, Arabic texts, Japanese and Chinese scrolls and treasures from the Middle East and Far East.

TEMPLE BAR

The section of Dublin between Dame Street and the Liffey is known as ★★ **Temple Bar**. The narrow streets with their 17th- to 19th-century houses were long neglected. When the municipal traffic authorities finally decided to adopt the long-postponed plan of building an enormous bus depot here during the 1980s they became aware that the area had become the centre of a thriving alternative scene, with shops, pubs and a lot of initiative. The Corporation then realised, albeit rather late in the day, that Temple Bar was popular not only with the locals but also with tourists. Today the entire area has been enthusiastically refurbished, but its former bohemianism has largely been swamped by commercialism.

The Temple Bar Information Centre, located at 18 Eustace Street, documents the history of the area. One real gem is the Irish Film Centre at 6 Eustace Street, which has two cinemas, an archive, bookshops, a bar, a restaurant and an excellent **Gallery of Photography**, all housed in an attractive building.

TRINITY COLLEGE

★★ **Trinity College ❷**, founded in 1592, is well worth a visit, especially its magnificent Old Library (open Mon–Sat 9.30am–5pm, Sun Oct–May noon–4.30pm, June–Sept 9.30am–4.30pm). Among the library's priceless treasures is the 9th-century ★★ *Book of Kells*, an illuminated manuscript of the Gospels that is a masterpiece of the ornate Hiberno-Saxon style. The book is thought to have been started at the Irish monastery on Iona in the 8th century and was completed at the monastery founded by St Columba at Kells in County Meath, north of Dublin. The breathtaking Long Room contains 200,000 of the college's oldest books, going back to Greek and Latin tracts, plus Ireland's oldest harp (probably 15th-century).

Trinity remained an exclusively Protestant university for most of its history, having been set up by Queen Elizabeth I to 'civilise' the Irish. Most of its buildings date from the 18th century.

In summer, students gather at the main entrance to the campus on College Green to offer guided tours of the university in return for a modest fee. These can be both informative and entertaining.

Star Attractions
● Temple Bar
● Trinity College

Below: Grafton Street shoppers
Bottom: Trinity College's Long Room Library

GRAFTON STREET

Grafton Street is a pedestrian precinct today, and along with the surrounding streets forms what is Dublin's most elegant (and most crowded) shopping quarter. The Powerscourt Townhouse Centre, for instance, was built inside an 18th-century townhouse. It has a roofed-over inner courtyard and numerous cafés, galleries and designer shops. Next to it, the **Civic Museum** (58 South William Street, currently closed for renovation) has plans, sketches and watercolours of Dublin – plus the damaged head of Admiral Lord Nelson from the O'Connell Street pillar blown up by the IRA in 1966 as their contribution to marking the 50th anniversary of the Easter Ris-

Map on page 22

*Below:the Custom House
Bottom: Stephen's Green
shopping centre*

ing. **Bewley's Oriental Café**, one of a chain dating to 1894, has great character.

At the south end of Grafton Street is ★★**St Stephen's Green ❸**, a 11-hectare (27-acre) park inhabited by nonchalant birdlife and containing statues of famous Dubliners. First-time visitors might enjoy a romantic orientation tour in a horse and carriage. Several of the Georgian buildings on the east side of the Green are modern replacements of the 18th-century originals.

NATIONAL MUSEUM AND GALLERY

Kildare Street is home to the ★★**National Museum ❹** (open Tues–Sat 10am–5pm, Sun 2–5pm), which has an impressive collection of Irish historical artefacts, including masterpieces of Celtic metalwork such as the Tara Brooch *(see picture, page 7)*.

Alongside European masters, the ★**National Gallery ❺** (Merrion Square, open Mon–Sat 9.30am–5.30pm, Thur until 8.30pm, Sun noon–5pm) also contains a collection of the most important Irish painters, including Jack B. Yeats. The Millennium Wing in Clare Street is a striking modern extension with an excellent restaurant and café.

Walk east past Trinity College, heading back towards the Liffey, and the impressive neoclassical architecture of the **Custom House ❻** comes

into view on the north bank; completed in 1791, it was a major centre of British power until it was gutted by fire in 1921 during the War of Independence. Today it contains government offices, but a visitor centre (mid-Mar–Oct Mon–Fri 10am–12.30pm, Sat–Sun 2–5pm; Nov–mid-Mar Wed–Fri 10am–12.30pm, Sun 2–5pm) gives access to some of its neoclassical rooms and staircases.

Nearby, **O'Connell Street** is the widest of the city's streets and home to numerous statues of Irish patriots. There have been recent attempts to improve it, but it has never quite recovered from its bombardment by British artillery during the 1916 Rising – memories of which are recalled by the bullet holes scarring the Ionic architecture of the **General Post Office**, where the rebels made a stand. A newer emblem of the city is the nearby **Spire of Dublin**, a 120-m (390-ft) stainless steel pillar erected in 2002. Henry Street and Moore Street, leading off O'Connell Street, are busy shopping areas; the latter accommodates Dublin's largest fruit and vegetable market, celebrated for its characterful stallholders.

PARNELL SQUARE

At the northern end of O'Connell Street is **Parnell Square ❼**. Two of the attractive townhouses at its northern end are museums. Charlemont House, built in 1762–65, contains the ★ **Dublin City Gallery, The Hugh Lane** (open Tues–Thur 9.30am–6pm, Fri–Sat until 5pm, Sun 11am–5pm), featuring an important collection of 19th- and 20th-century European art and work by contemporary Irish artists such as Michael Farrell and Robert Ballagh. In 1998 the gallery painstakingly dismantled the London studio of the Dublin-born artist Francis Bacon and faithfully reconstructed it here.

Number 18 contains the ★★ **Dublin Writers' Museum** (open Mon–Sat 10am–5pm, Sun 11am–5pm; June–Aug Mon–Fri until 6pm). Opened in 1991, it features the memorabilia of such icons as Swift, Yeats, Shaw, Joyce, O'Casey and Beckett. There is a reading room, bookshop and café.

Star Attractions
● **St Stephen's Green**
● **National Museum**
● **Dublin Writers' Museum**

Below: statue of labour leader James Larkin outside the General Post Office
Bottom: window in Dublin Writers' Museum

Map on page 22

COURTS AND CORPSES

Go to the west of the square and retrace your steps southwards down Dorset Street. Soon Henrietta Street appears with its former noble residences. At the end are the **King's Inns ❽**, the impressive-looking neoclassical law court buildings that are the envy of many other cities. They were designed by James Gandon, whose more famous work north of the Liffey includes the Custom House and the imposing **Four Courts ❾** on Inns Quay, built between 1786 and 1802 and housing Ireland's High Court (for public admission times, tel: 888 6000).

Below: mummified corpses in St Michan's Church
Bottom: Guinness Storehouse

Northward along Church Street from the Four Courts is ★ **St Michan's**, dating from 1095, although the present much restored building dates from the 17th century. It is notable for its underground vaults where mummified corpses, brown and leathery, have been preserved in the dry air.

DRINKERS' DUBLIN

Not far from the courts are the various monuments to alcohol consumption in Dublin. In Bow Street, to the west of the Four Courts, the **Old Jameson Distillery ❿** (open daily 9.30am–5.30pm; tours run continuously) is a visitors' centre, shop and museum. If you walk a short way along the river down Arran/Ellis Quay and then cross the Rory O'Moore Bridge, you'll find yourself face to face with the enormous **Guinness Brewery**. The place itself can't be visited, but there's a brewery museum, the ★★ **Guinness Storehouse ⓫** (daily Sept– June 9.30am–5pm, July–Aug 9.30am–9pm) on nearby Crane Street. It traces the brewery's history and a video shows how the stout is produced. A glass of Guinness is included in the entry fee.

Nearby, the picturesque old quarter where the Guinness workers used to live, known as **The Liberties** – so called because it once stood outside the medieval city walls and so was beyond the Lord Mayor's jurisdiction. The area contains many antiques shops, especially along Francis Street.

ST PATRICK'S CATHEDRAL

At the southern end of Francis Street, on the left, is ★★ **St Patrick's Cathedral** ⓬. Construction work began on the cathedral in the 12th century, but in its present Gothic form it dates from 1220–70, with several later additions. Today it is the national cathedral of the Curch of Ireland. Jonathan Swift, poet and author of *Gulliver's Travels*, was dean here from 1713 to 1745. His tombstone is at the foot of the second column to the right of the main portal. The inscription on the plaque behind it is Swift's own epitaph: *Abi, viator, et imitare, si poteris, strenuum pro virili libertatis vindicatorem* ('Go, traveller, and imitate, if you can, one who strove with all his strength to champion liberty').

Bull Alley Street by the Cathedral is the departure point for Viking Splash Tours, which will show you Dublin by land and water in reconditioned World War II amphibious vehicles.

CHRIST CHURCH

Patrick Street leads in the direction of the Liffey to the city's second medieval cathedral, ★ **Christ Church Cathedral** ⓭, which is used by the Church of Ireland. Built between 1173 and 1220, it was renovated and extended in 1875.

To find out more about the two cathedrals and the development of the city, visit the **Dublinia**

Star Attractions
● Guinness Storehouse
● St Patrick's Cathedral

Below: plaque on St Patrick's Cathedral
Bottom: Christ Church

Map on page 22

Wellington Monument
This 60-metre (200-ft) obelisk inside the main entrance to Phoenix Park was erected in tribute to the Dublin-born general. But Wellington played down his Irish origins: 'Just because you were born in a stable doesn't make you a horse.'

Parnell's grave in Glasnevin Cemetery

exhibition opposite Christ Church in Synod Hall (open Apr–Sept daily 10am–5pm; Oct–Mar Mon–Sat 11am–4pm, Sun 10am–4.30pm) where there are models and videos. Guided tours of the cathedral are organised from here.

OUTER DUBLIN

About 2.5km (1½ miles) west of O'Connell Bridge is the gloomy grey bulk of ★ **Kilmainham Jail** (Apr–Sept 9.30am–4.45pm; Oct–Mar 9.30am–4pm Mon–Fri, closed Sat, 10am–4.45pm Sun), intimately associated with Ireland's struggle for independence. The '1916 corridor' contains the cells where the captured leaders of the Easter Rising awaited the execution that would transform them into martyrs, and a museum focuses on 19th-century notions of crime, punishment and reform.

To its east, the former Kilmainham Royal Hospital now houses the **Irish Museum of Modern Art** (Tues–Sat 10am–5.30pm, Sun noon–5.30pm), which has a patchy collection but interesting temporary exhibitions. To the north, across the Liffey, is **Phoenix Park**, at 712 hectares (1,760 acres) more than five times the size of London's Hyde Park and twice as big as New York's Central Park. Nearby is **Dublin Zoo**, the world's third oldest public zoo, noted for its breeding of lions (it claims to have bred the lion that introduced MGM movies).

Another worthwhile excursion is to the northern suburb of Glasnevin, where the ★ **National Botanic Gardens** (Mar–Oct Mon–Sat 9am–6pm, Sun 10am–6pm; Nov–Feb Mon–Sat 10am– 4.30pm, Sun 11am–4.30pm; bus Nos. 13 and 19) has a variety of plant life and 19th-century greenhouses.

Adjoining the gardens to the southwest is the ★ **Glasnevin Cemetery**, where some of the most important figures in recent Irish history are buried. Here lie the tombs of Charles Stewart Parnell, Daniel O'Connell, Éamon de Valera, the actress Maud Gonne MacBride (1865–1953) who founded the 'Daughters of Ireland' women's movement, and her son Sean MacBride (1904–88), an IRA leader who became chairman of Amnesty International and won the Nobel Peace Prize.

2: The East

**Dublin – Drogheda – Newgrange – Navan –
Mullingar – Athlone – Kildare – Wicklow –
Wexford (approx 500km/300 miles)**

Map on page 32

Many people visit the famous sights on this route
from Dublin and then go straight off to the west coast
to discover what they think is the 'real' Ireland.
Counties such as Meath, Cavan or Offaly, and every-
day Irish life away from the major routes remain a
closed book to them. This route leads northwest-
wards from Dublin and into the interior before going
round the capital in a broad arc to the west and
returning to the coast again in the southeast.

*Below: cottage in Co. Meath
Bottom: peckish ponies by the
region's drystone walls*

THE GREEN INTERIOR

Some of the most important sights in Ireland are
to be found along this stretch, but the route also
passes through miles of undramatic green landscape with farmhouses, low hills and peat bogs.
As Dublin continues to grow, commuters are
moving ever further from the centre, bringing
most locations within an hour's drive of the city
into the commuter belt. New roads and housing
are transforming a hitherto sleepy rural landscape.

That doesn't mean there's nothing to visit,
though. Far from it: located between Drogheda
and Navan are the most impressive megalithic

Map below

tombs in Europe, and Clonmacnoise to the south of Athlone is a spectacular Early Christian site.

There is no shortage of sports opportunities along the way either: you can fish in the Boyne or the Slaney rivers, go riding in Kildare or Wicklow, and play golf at Portmarnock or Mount Juliet. The southern section of the route also passes by some particularly attractive sandy beaches, situated in the part of Ireland that benefits from the most sunshine and the least rain.

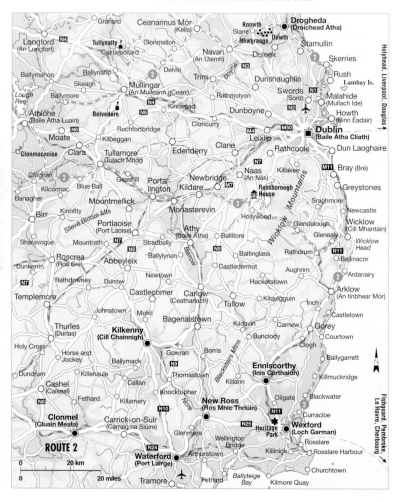

HOWTH

Howth is the northern terminus of the Dublin suburban railway (DART). Before the town, the gardens of Howth Castle with their famous rhododendrons appear on the left (the castle itself is not open to the public). The attractive little town itself, with its streets sloping steeply down towards the river, has a prosperous look about it: the formerly important ferry harbour is used today as a yachting harbour.

There are boat excursions from Howth out to the island bird sanctuary **Ireland's Eye**, where passengers disembark next to a 'Martello tower', a round coastal fort. These forts were constructed at the beginning of the 19th century when the British feared an attack by Napoleon Bonaparte, and great numbers of them survive around the coast of Ireland. The tower is the only building on the island apart from the forlorn ruins of a 6th-century monastery; the rest of the island is occupied by vast flocks of seabirds.

Howth's fine fish
The largest fishing fleet in Ireland sails out of Howth. There are several local restaurants that take advantage of their catch, fresh off the boats. One of them, King Sitric *(see page 115)*, ranks alongside the most famous in the country.

Malahide Castle

MALAHIDE CASTLE

The R106 leads north from Howth along the magnificent coastline to reach ★ **Malahide Castle** (open Apr–Oct Mon–Sat 10am–5pm, Sun 11am–6pm; Nov–Mar Mon–Fri 10am–5pm, Sat and Sun 2–5pm). This was the seat of the Anglo-Norman family of Talbot de Malahide from 1185 until the 1970s. Most of the present structure dates from the 14th to the 17th centuries.

After the death of the last Lord Talbot, the castle was taken over by Dublin County Council, and today it contains portraits from the National Gallery collection, including masterpieces by Hogarth, Lely, Romney and Van Dyck. The botanical garden, laid out more than 50 years ago over 8 hectares (19 acres), contains over 5,000 species, including exotic plants from Australasia and South America.

On the way northwards it's worth taking the minor roads along the coast as far as **Skerries**. This popular seaside resort has a long sandy beach, and there's a good walk across the cliffs south to the fishing village of Loughshinny. There

Map on page 32

Stallions in the sand
The road to Drogheda leads via Bettystown (where the Celtic Tara Brooch was found on the seashore, *see page 26*) and Laytown, which is renowned for the only horse races in Europe that are officially held on a beach. The races are held on one day in July or August at low tide.

are several small islands off the coast that can either be reached from Skerries by boat or – only after finding out exactly when the times are – on foot at low tide.

DROGHEDA

The large town and port of **Drogheda** lies on the Boyne river, 5km (3 miles) inland from where it meets the Irish Sea. As you enter the suburbs, it is abundantly clear that Drogheda is an industrial centre, but the picturesque little streets and alleys in the old town have hardly changed since medieval times. The area around West Street and Lawrence Street to the north of the Boyne is well worth a visit.

To the south of the river is the **Millmount**, which probably originated as a prehistoric burial mound. A Norman fortress on the hill had to make way for a Martello tower and a garrison in 1808; today the Millmount has several crafts shops, a restaurant and also a municipal museum documenting Drogheda's turbulent history (open Mon–Sat 10am–5pm, Sun 2–5pm). There's a good view from the top of the tower across the town to the Boyne Valley beyond.

The head of a martyred archbishop, Oliver Plunkett, is preserved in St Peter's Church, Drogheda

BATTLE OF THE BOYNE

About 8km (5 miles) west of Drogheda, the road to Slane (N51) passes the site of the Battle of the Boyne. The place is known today as **Oldbridge**, because of the bridge over the river; the battlefield is marked by the stump of an obelisk. After England's Catholic king, James II, was deposed in 1688 during the so-called 'Glorious Revolution' against his autocratic rule, and replaced by his daughter Mary and her Dutch husband William III of Orange, James embarked for Ireland supported by French troops. James hoped he could drive out the Protestant settlers and use a newly-strengthened Catholic Ireland as a base from which to regain his crown.

On 1 July 1690 William of Orange defeated him at the Boyne. The Battle of the Boyne has assumed a symbolic character for the Protestants of Northern Ireland: the anniversary is celebrated by the Orange Order each 12 July with marches.

PALACE ON THE BOYNE

A few miles further west, the past really makes an impact with the impressive prehistoric graves of ★★★ **Newgrange**, **Knowth** and **Dowth**, located on a bend in the river. Access is through the new **Brú na Bóinne Visitor Centre** (open Mar, Apr and Oct daily 9.30am–5.30pm, May and Sept 9am–6.30pm, June–Aug 9am–7pm, Nov–Feb 9.30am–5pm). The collection of 5,000-year-old graves here has been known since Celtic times as *Brú na Bóinne*, or the 'Palace on the Boyne'.

NEWGRANGE

The burial mound of Newgrange, the most interesting of the three main grave sites, is part of a group of between 28 and 40 corridor tombs in the valley of the Boyne. Newgrange itself dates from around 3100BC, which makes it older than Stonehenge or the pyramids of Giza, and one of the most important stone monuments in Europe.

The mound is almost pear-shaped; it is about 90m (300ft) across and 14m (45ft) high. The outer edge is lined with 97 stone slabs, and 16m (52ft)

Star Attraction
● Newgrange

Below: the old town walls in Drogheda
Bottom: Newgrange

Map
on page
32

Solstice at Newgrange
Newgrange is one of the most popular places in the world to see the winter solstice. The waiting list to view the phenomenon from the burial chamber is currently 10 years long. A lottery system has been introduced to select spectators.

Entrance to a burial chamber at Newgrange

further away there once stood a circle of 38 menhirs, each 2.5-m (9-ft) high. Twelve survive. The tomb contains a 19-m (60-ft) long corridor, 1m (3ft) wide and 2m (6ft) high. The burial chamber itself has a vaulted ceiling almost 6m (20ft) high at its centre, made of megalithic slabs that have been fitted together with such precision that water cannot enter. Three side-chambers curve off the main chamber in the shape of a cross; a hollowed-out stone basin containing human remains was discovered in each.

The function of the stone across the entrance was a mystery for years – it contains a slit 20cm (8 inches) wide – until research by the archaeologist Michael O'Kelly in 1969 revealed that the first rays of the morning sun on the winter solstice (21 December) shine through the crack and along the corridor to the burial chamber.

Many of the stones are ornately decorated with double spirals, concentric semicircles and rhomboid shapes. The Stone Age people of Europe were clearly far less primitive than is generally supposed. As for the other tombs, archaeologists are subjecting Knowth to closer scrutiny, which is why only part of the site may be open. The grave is believed to be around 500 years older, and possibly more complex, than Newgrange.

To the west of Knowth is the beautiful old village of **Slane**. On the outskirts, the **Hill of Slane**, where St Patrick proclaimed Christianity in 433, has the ruins of a 16th-century church. The view over the plain is striking.

HILL OF TARA

The town of **Navan** is a busy industrial and administrative centre, but south of the town one is transported back to the age of Celtic myths and legends. The ★ **Hill of Tara** (visitors' centre open May–Oct daily 10am–6pm; guided tours) is reputedly where the high kings of Ireland had their palace. Indeed, ruins of a Bronze Age fort lie beneath the grass and the hill is surrounded by earthworks. Excavations have revealed that an enormous wooden hall may once have stood here. The view of the surrounding landscape from the top of the hill is rewarding, though it must be emphasised that very little of this place's glorious past can be seen today and one has to rely on the interpretations and explanations provided during the guided tour.

The tours begin at the former Protestant church (now the visitors' centre) and lead past earthworks and ditches with names such as *Rath na Riogh* (Wall of the Kings), *Dumha Na nGiall* (Ditch of the Hostages) or *Teach Cormaic* (Cormac's House). Much is made of the possible link with the most famous of Ireland's high kings, Cormac Mac Art, who ruled in the 3rd century AD and, so legend has it, surrounded himself with a court of bards, artists and heroes.

DUNSANY CASTLE

Directly south of the Hill of Tara is **Dunsany Castle** (guided tours May–July; tel: 046-902 6202). The oldest section dates from 1180. Since the 15th century the castle has been the seat of the Dunsany family. Edward John Moreton Drax Plunkett, the 18th Baron Dunsany (1878–1957), is renowned as *the* Lord Dunsany, the novelist, playwright and poet, whose stories have been translated into many languages. In Ireland he was best known for his plays, written at W. B. Yeats's request for the Abbey Theatre in Dublin.

Below: the Hill of Slane, where St Patrick introduced Christianity to Ireland
Bottom: entrance to the Hill of Tara

Map on page 32

Mac Art's troops
The fighting soldiers of Cormaic Mac Art, Ireland's 3rd-century high king, were known as *fianna*. Many nationalist groups have since borrowed the term, including the 19th-century American exile organisation known as the Fenians, the Na Fianna Éireann republican youth movement, and the current Fianna Fáil party.

Portrait of Christ from the Book of Kells, kept in Trinity College, Dublin

KELLS

Travel westwards from Dunsany along minor roads as far as the ruins of **Bective Abbey**. This Cistercian abbey was founded in 1147, and the remains date from the 16th century.

It was at ★ **Kells** (Ceanannus Mór) that Christianity in Ireland reached a high point. In AD550 St Columba (the missionary who brought Christianity to Scotland) founded the monastery west of today's town centre. From 800 onwards the famous illuminated manuscript was created which came to be known as the *Book of Kells*. It can be admired in the library of Trinity College, Dublin *(see page 24)*.

The cemetery of the small Protestant church contains a 30-m (100-ft) high tower which formed a part of the monastery built before 1076. There are several Celtic crosses in the vicinity, the best-preserved of which is more than 3m (11ft) high and decorated with biblical scenes.

MULLINGAR AND SURROUNDINGS

The dignified little market town of ★ **Mullingar** lies in a region of rolling hills and tiny lakes, on a bend in the Royal Canal. The latter was built as a waterway connecting Dublin and the Shannon at the end of the 18th century, but it went out of commercial use around 1880. The overgrown riverbank is popular with hikers, and the calm waters are ideal for rowing boats and canoes. The lakes and rivers around Mullingar are also an angler's paradise, and fishing competitions are held annually on Lough Owel; trout are caught in April and August, pike in June.

To the south of Mullingar is **Belvedere House** (open daily Apr–Aug 10.30am–7pm, Sept–Oct closes 6.30pm, Nov–Mar closes 4.30pm). The house was built in the Palladian style in 1740. Entrance to the house is though the servants' quarters, showing life behind the scenes. The 65 hectares (160 acres) of lakeside estate can be toured on the Belvedere Tram.

To the north of Mullingar, **Tullynally Castle** (gardens open May–Aug 2–6pm) is an impressive, turreted castle. Originally built in the 17th century, it underwent extensive alterations around 1800. The house, home to the historian and tree-lover, Thomas Pakenham, is closed, but the parkland, laid out in 1760, and gardens are well worth visiting.

Star Attraction
● Clonmacnoise

ATHLONE AND CLONMACNOISE

The town of **Athlone** itself is rather a dreary place, and gains most of its attraction from being situated astride the largest river in Ireland. The most important building is the 13th-century **Athlone Castle**, on the west bank of the Shannon beside the main bridge. The fortress houses the Castle Museum (open May–Sept daily 10am–5pm), with exhibitions on local history. Athlone has a cabin cruiser hire centre for trips along the Shannon.

The magnificent monastery complex at ★★ **Clonmacnoise** (open daily mid-June–Sept 9am–7pm, Oct–May 10am–6pm or dusk; guided tours from visitors' centre/museum), is situated at the geographical centre of Ireland. Follow signs to the south from Athlone (24km/14 miles).

As you approach the complex along the river from Athlone, the long silhouette of an Ice-Age moraine comes into view across to the right, followed by a ruin surrounded by earthworks –

Below: church at Mullingar
Bottom: ruins at Clonmacnoise

Map
on page
32

Cruise to Clonmacnoise
The most attractive way to reach Clonmacnoise is by boat along the River Shannon. In summer, excursions depart from Athlone at 10am.

*Cross of the Scriptures
and O'Rourke's Tower
at Clonmacnoise*

all that remains of a castle built by Bishop John de Grey in the 13th century. Beyond it, between the trees, the two round towers of the monastery itself can be seen. From the 7th to the 12th centuries, Clonmacnoise was the cultural and spiritual centre of the Celtic church. An inventory drawn up after a serious fire in 1179 mentions 106 houses and 13 churches on the site.

Today, alongside the round towers, the ruins of a cathedral and eight churches can be seen, as well as three Celtic crosses and around 200 funerary slabs. Most of the remains date from the 10th to 12th centuries. After the 13th century the site lost its importance, and when the English destroyed it in 1552 it was only a minor bishopric. **Shannonbridge** (7km/4 miles) south of Athlone is the nearest village to the Bord na Mona Bog Rail Tour at *Uisce Dubh*. A small locomotive pulls one carriage slowly across the bogland on a narrow gauge railway while the driver gives a commentary on the flora and fauna of the Irish peat bog (Apr–Oct daily 10am–5pm).

TULLAMORE

Southeast of Athlone is **Tullamore**. The centre of this small town was largely rebuilt at the end of the 18th century after a crash landing by a hot-air balloon in 1785 started a major fire which destroyed more than 100 houses. Tullamore is noted for producing *Tullamore Dew Whiskey* and the liqueur *Irish Mist*. You can sample the whiskey at the 18th-century Locke's Distillery in **Kilbeggan**, 11km (7 miles) to the north of Tullamore (open Apr–Oct daily 9am–6pm, Nov–Mar 10am–4pm).

South of the town is **Charleville Castle** (open Apr and May Sat–Sun 11am–5pm; June–Sept Wed–Sun 11am–5pm; guided tours), built between 1800 and 1812, and often considered the Irish equivalent of mad King Ludwig's Neuschwanstein castle in Bavaria. This neo-Gothic edifice is made up of all kinds of stylistic borrowings. Commissioned by the wealthy landowner Charles William Bury, later Lord

Tullamore and Earl of Charleville, it was designed by the architect Francis Johnston.

KILDARE

About 48km (30 miles) to the east is ★ **Kildare**, the centre of the Irish racehorse-breeding business. The **National Stud**, out on the vast expanse of the Curragh, can be inspected (guided tours mid-Feb–mid-Nov daily 9.30am–6pm), and the admission fee also includes a visit to the **Japanese Garden** that was laid out by the stud's founder, Colonel William Hall Walker (later Lord Wavertree) in the early 20th century. The stables form part of the tour, as does a museum with displays documenting the history of the horse and its development in Ireland. One of the most eye-catching exhibits is the skeleton of the Irish-bred Grand National winner, Arkle.

Below: Kildare's Japanese Garden
Bottom: the Curragh racetrack

CURRAGH RACETRACK

The nearby **Curragh Racetrack** hosts one of the most renowned races in Ireland every June, the Irish Derby. There are several other race meetings here from May to September each year, including the 2,000 Guineas and the St Leger. The Irish daily newspapers carry details of race meetings across the country (there are about 280 each year).

Map
on page
32

Peatland World
To the east of Tullamore, the route passes along the southern edge of the Bog of Allan. In Lullymore, near Rathangan, Peatland World can be visited (open Mon–Fri 10am–5pm, Sat–Sun 2–6pm). Video films and guided tours provide an introduction to the flora, fauna, geology and archaeology of the moor.

Harvesting peat in County Wicklow

Every country track in the Kildare region seems to have a stud farm at the end of it; motorists should take care on bends because there are riders everywhere. Groups of horses doing their morning training on the Curragh can be seen from the N7, the main road to Dublin – a particularly impressive sight in the early morning mist.

RUSSBOROUGH HOUSE

The most direct and also the most attractive route to the east coast via the Wicklow Mountains begins in the small town of Hollywood on the N81. Before setting off for the mountains, visit ★ **Russborough House** just north of the town, one of the best-preserved Palladian country houses in Ireland (open May–Sept daily 10.30am–5.30pm, Apr and Oct Sun only 10.30am–5.30pm).

The house was built by the Irish architect Richard Castle for Joseph Leeson, who later became Earl of Milltown. Today it is owned by the Beit family, and exhibits from their art foundation are displayed inside. Several spectacular burglaries led to much of the collection being made over to the National Gallery in Dublin in 1988, but what remains is indeed impressive: there are works by Boucher, Gainsborough, Reynolds, Teniers and Rubens, as well as four Joseph Vernets painted especially for the house and set into the stucco of the drawing room.

GLENDALOUGH

About 1km (½ mile) to the north of Russborough House, turn right on to the R758, and at the Poulaphouca Reservoir – the source of most of Dublin's water – travel as far as the junction with the R756, which rises slowly towards Wicklow Gap. On the other side of the pass a road branches right, signposted to ★★ **Glendalough** – the name means 'valley of the two lakes'. The beautiful landscape combined with the Early Christian monastery make this a very special site. It's tempting to wish away the hundreds of visitors and to be alone with the sounds that St Kevin must have heard when he came here in the 6th century. From the 10th to the 12th centuries, Glendalough was second in importance only to Clonmacnoise as a centre of culture and pilgrimage.

Most of the surviving buildings date from that time, including a 33-m (110-ft) high round tower and the remains of seven chapels. One of the earliest finds was made near the upper lake: about 10m (30ft) above the shoreline is the entrance to a small cave, referred to as 'St Kevin's Bed', though its first inhabitants were there 2,000 years or so before Kevin. The monastery has had quite a violent history: between 775 and 1070, despite its location up in the mountains, it was attacked on at least four occasions by the Vikings. Later, in 1398, it was almost completely destroyed by English troops. If the place looks familiar, it could be because you saw the film *Braveheart*: Glendalough was used for the wedding scene.

WICKLOW

Wicklow is a pleasant small town and harbour. On the rocks above the beach just south of the town, the remains of Black Castle can be seen. It was built by the FitzGeralds from Wales in 1178 as part of their harbour fortifications against attacks by the O'Byrne and O'Toole clans. There are several beach walks to the south of Wicklow

Star Attraction
● Glendalough

Below: round tower at Glendalough
Bottom: near St Kevin's Monastery, Glendalough

Head and the sandy beach extends for miles as far as Brittas Bay. From the coast road the sea view is obscured by endless rows of caravans.

WEXFORD

Continue south along the coast, via Arklow (ship-building, fertilisers), the holiday resort of Courtown Harbour and the sand dunes on Curracloe Beach, as far as ★ **Wexford**. Many of Wexford's historical buildings no longer exist, but this friendly town more than makes up for that with its atmosphere. Main Street, which runs parallel to the harbour, is very lively, especially when the pubs fill up in the evening – Wexford has an astonishing number of pubs. The quays here have been silent since the harbour basin was silted up. The red sandstone Westgate Tower is the only remaining of five fortified gateways in the Norman town walls.

Irish National Heritage Park, Wexford

The **Wexford Opera Festival**, each October, has a reputation for staging relatively little-known operas performed by superb casts and orchestras. The entire town joins in, too, with street theatre, poetry recitals and live music in the pubs.

Four km (2 miles) to the northwest of Wexford, along the N11, is the **Irish National Heritage Park** (open Mar–Oct daily 9.30am–6.30pm, last admission one hour before closing; Nov–Feb daily 9.30am– 5.30pm; guided tours). This open-air museum documents Irish history from prehistoric times to the arrival of the Anglo-Normans. Skilful reconstructions of Stone and Bronze Age huts, an Early Christian monastery, a Viking longboat (on the Slaney river, which flows through the site) and a Norman fortress provide an insight into what life was like in the different ages. Every-day trades, such as baking or blacksmithing, are also on display in special exhibitions.

About 15km (9 miles) to the south of Wexford is the holiday resort of **Rosslare Strand**, which is very popular for its sandy beach. From here it is only another 5km (3 miles) to **Rosslare Harbour**, where ferries depart for Fishguard, Pembroke, Le Havre and Cherbourg.

3: The South

Kilkenny – Cashel – Clonmel – Waterford – Tramore – Youghal – Cork (approx 260km/ 160 miles)

Star Attraction
● Kilkenny

Every route along the south coast leads through picturesque villages and past idyllic stretches of coastline. Further inland, County Tipperary has luxuriant grazing land and a number of ancient ruins, some of them 1,000 years old. The south of Ireland is very thinly populated, and would be even emptier were it not for the success of tourism. Even today, the landscape is an easy one to get lost in, far from the madding crowd.

This route leads from Kilkenny through County Tipperary and then south to Waterford, from where it follows the coast to Cork.

KILKENNY

★★ **Kilkenny** is an attractive town with evidence of its medieval past. Before the Normans built their fortress here in the 12th century, settlement was concentrated around the monastery founded 600 years earlier. In Irish it is known as *Cill Chainnigh*, meaning 'Church of St Cainneach'. Canice, as the saint is known in English, gave her name to the second-largest cathedral in Ireland: the ★ **Cathedral of St Canice**, built between 1202 and 1260. It contains

Why worry?
The following Irish philosophy is often printed on linen teatowels and other souvenirs: 'There are only two things to worry about: either you are well or you are sick. If you are well, then there is nothing to worry about. But if you are sick, there are two things to worry about: either you will get well or you will die. If you get well, then there is nothing to worry about. If you die, there are only two things to worry about: either you will go to heaven or to hell. If you go to heaven, there is nothing to worry about. But if you go to hell, you'll be so damn busy shaking hands with friends, you won't have time to worry. Why worry?'

Holycross Abbey, Kilkenny

the impressive double tomb of Piers Butler, 8th Earl of Ormonde, and his wife – it is one of the finest medieval tomb monuments in Ireland.

The noble family had its seat from 1391 to 1935 at ★ **Kilkenny Castle** (open 10.30am–4pm; tours every hour from 11am). The castle, surrounded by parkland, towers above the River Nore, just to the south of the town centre. Its oldest sections date from 1192, but it was altered extensively in the 17th and 19th centuries. The buildings form three sides of a square, and there is a fine view of parkland from the open side to the southeast. The 'Long Gallery' in the northeast wing has a remarkable collection of Butler family portraits. In the castle cellar there is an art gallery with several modern works.

DESIGN CENTRE

The Castle Stables on the opposite side of Castle Road contain the **Kilkenny Design Centre** (open daily 9am–5pm; Jan–Mar closed Sun), which actively promotes Irish arts and crafts. The workshops are well worth a visit. There is a shop and a restaurant, too.

Piers Butler

Had things turned out differently, Piers Butler, whose seat was Kilkenny Castle, would have been the father-in-law of Anne Boleyn. In an effort to bring the Earl of Ormonde title back to his family, Sir Thomas Boleyn arranged a marriage between Anne and Sir Piers Butler's son. The marriage was a shambles and soon ended in separation, but it had a much less messy finale than Anne's more famous relationship with Henry VIII.

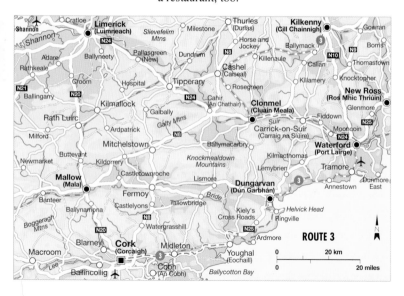

KILKENNY CITY CENTRE

High Street and Parliament Street run north from the foot of the castle mound towards the cathedral. With their many little side streets, they make up what is the most attractive part of the old town.

Built in 1594, the **Shee Alms House** (open Mon–Sat 9am–6pm, until 5pm Nov–Mar), is of historical as well as architectural interest. It contains the tourist information office on the ground floor. On the first floor a scale model of the old town documents local history.

The 18th-century **Town Hall** in the High Street has an upper storey that juts out above the street, forming an arcade. The building is made of locally quarried black stone. ★ **Rothe House** (Mar–Nov Mon–Sat 10.30am–5pm, Sun 3–5pm; Dec–Feb Mon–Sat 1–5pm) is a merchant's townhouse dating from the end of the 16th century. It was constructed around several courtyards. The building and its interior are of more interest than the municipal history museum it houses.

Go through Kilkenny's **Black Freren Gate** – the last surviving town gate – to **Black Abbey**. Founded in 1225, the abbey was named after the Dominican Order's black habits. The existing building is largely from the 19th century.

THROUGH THE GOLDEN VALE

From Kilkenny, drive along the southern edge of the Slieveardagh hills (slieve, or *sliabh*, means mountain), through Tipperary with its hedge-lined meadows. This broad fertile valley, which extends southeastwards from Limerick to Clonmel, is known as the 'Golden Vale'. Life is prosperous here at the heart of Ireland's largest cattle breeding and dairy farming region, and cattle markets are a regular event even in the smallest villages.

ROCK OF CASHEL

As you approach one of these towns, Cashel, you will see the spectacular ★★ **Rock of Cashel** (open

Below: modern crafts on show at Kilkenny
Bottom: design has always played a prominent part in advertising the national brew

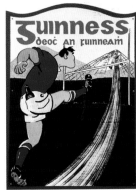

Below and bottom: the Rock of Cashel

mid-Sept–mid-Mar daily 9am–4.30pm; mid-Mar–mid-June until 5.30pm; mid-June–mid-Sept until 7pm). A limestone crag looms above the plain. On top of it, silhouetted against the sky, is one of the most remarkable ruins in Ireland, those of **St Patrick's Cathedral**.

The entrance is on the south side, and leads into the 15th-century Hall of the Vicars' Choral, which contains a small museum and a 20-minute audio-visual introduction to the history of the complex. If you step out of the hall you'll find yourself face to face with the south transept of the monumental Gothic cathedral, which was begun in 1235. It was restored at great expense in 1495 after Count Gerald of Kildare set fire to it in an attempt to incinerate the archbishop.

From 1750 onwards the church fell into decay. It is said that the Protestant bishop of that time was too lazy to walk up the hill, which was too steep for his horse-drawn coach. The round tower on the corner of the north transept is probably 11th-century in origin, and is the oldest structure on the hill. It also shows how cleverly the cathedral builders combined their additions with what was already in existence.

The rock plays host to the Cashel Cultural Festival every July. The event makes the ruins a picturesque backdrop for Irish music, theatre and craft fairs (tel: 062-62511).

CORMAC'S CHAPEL

At first glance, **Cormac's Chapel** seems to be a diagonal extension between the choir and the transept, but on closer observation it turns out to be the best-preserved Romanesque structure in Ireland, 100 years older than the cathedral itself. The decoration, which shows influences from Bavaria and Alsace, is a fine example of the artistic skill of the stonemasons during that period.

Naturally, a set of buildings as important as this has its fair share of legends. St Patrick is said to have converted the king of Munster to Christianity here in the 5th century, and baptised him. When the Saint's crozier pierced the King's foot he did not complain, thinking it was part of the ceremony.

Star Attraction
● Rock of Cashel

Old Books
Cashel's Bolton Library, in the grounds of St John's Protestant Cathedral, has more than 12,000 volumes, specialising in history and theology. It includes 'the smallest book in the world' and has a collection of silver from 1585 on.

CASHEL'S CULTURAL CENTRE

★ **Cashel** itself, at the foot of the rock, is an attractive little town with several good restaurants. **Brú Ború**,(craft shop open year around; evening performances begin at 9pm Tues–Sat) a cultural centre where music and dance shows are performed during summer, is also worth visiting for a flavour of Tipperary life. The Cashel Heritage Centre (open 9.30am–5.30pm daily) at the town hall invites visitors to explore the town's rich ecclesiastical heritage. A scale model of Cashel in the 1640s highlights treasures often over shadowed by 'The Rock'.

Brú Ború heritage centre, Cashel

CLONMEL

Further along the route, nestling among magnificent landscape on the River Suir, the small and prosperous town of **Clonmel** is the 'dog capital' of Ireland. It has the country's foremost greyhound racing track. The races are usually held on Thursday. Anyone keen to experience the sport should go along as it's a particularly good way to meet the locals. Check the local paper for times.

The town's other claim to fame is that the novelist Laurence Sterne was born here *(see box, page 50)* and it was once the home of Anthony Trollope. Every September a literary festival is held

Map on page 46

to celebrate these connections. St Mary's Church and the town walls date back to the 13th century and withstood a three-week siege by Oliver Cromwell in 1650.

Laurence Sterne
Born in 1713 in Clonmel, the novelist Laurence Sterne was educated at Cambridge and entered the Anglican Church. He moved to London in 1760. In the same year, the first volume of his masterpiece *Tristram Shandy* was published. Its denunciation by many on moral and literary grounds served to promote its popular success. Eight subsequent volumes followed in addition to an unfinished manuscript, *A Sentimental Journey*, about his travels through France and Italy. He died in 1768.

COMERAGH MOUNTAINS

Clonmel is a good base for hiking trips and cycle tours across the ★ **Comeragh Mountains** to the south. The tourist information office on Sarsfield Street has useful maps and brochures to guide hikers to the various peaks. The highest point in the Comeraghs is **Fascoum** at 789m (2,590ft). Motorists can turn off the main road from Clonmel to Dungarvan at Ballymacarbry and then follow the course of the River Nire into the mountains. To see the goats and other wildlife here, you would have to walk or cycle rather than drive.

ORMONDE CASTLE

There's a strange-looking castle in the market town of **Carrick-on-Suir**. ★ **Ormonde Castle** (open June–Sept daily 9.30am–6.30pm) is situated at the east end of Castle Street and dates from the 15th century. The 10th earl of Ormonde (known as 'Black Tom'), a favourite of Queen Elizabeth I, attached a Tudor-style manor house to the castle, and the result is unique in Ireland. Normally such houses were only built in peaceful England. Here, in war-torn Ireland, defensive precautions had to be taken, hence the arrow slits just above the main entrance, which are an unusual feature in a Tudor house.

Carrick-on-Suir's castle

WATERFORD

★★ **Waterford** is a friendly place on the south bank of the River Suir, 6km (4 miles) above its junction with the Barrow at the head of Waterford Harbour. The charming old town centre is encircled by one of the best-preserved medieval walls in Ireland. Beyond lie the less attractive suburban housing and industrial estates of this town of 42,500 people.

Vikings founded a settlement here in the 9th century, which they named *Vadrafjord*. Reginald's Tower, built in 1003 by Reginald the Norseman, stands high above the river at the eastern end of the town wall. Today it houses the **Civic Museum** (open Mar and Oct daily 10am–5pm; Apr–Sept 9.30am–6.30pm), which contains interesting collections relating to local history.

The ★ **Waterford Treasures at the Granary** (open daily May and Sept 9.30am–6pm, June–Aug 9.30am–9pm, Oct–Apr 10am–5pm) features an extensive range of rare and beautiful artefacts from the Waterford region. Technological innovations bring the past to life with a moving Viking ship presentation and humorous news broadcasts about the city's history up to the 19th century.

Waterford is one of Ireland's major trading harbours and modern freighters dock along the quays. The rows of pastel-coloured houses edging the river add a picturesque touch. There are two important churches in the old part of the town, both designed by the architect John Roberts: the **Holy Trinity Cathedral** in Barronstrand Street, a dignified-looking Georgian structure built in 1792, and the neoclassical **Christ Church Cathedral**, which he designed in 1772 for the Church of Ireland. The square in front of the latter, **Cathedral Square**, with its magnificent 18th-century townhouses, is the finest in Waterford.

Star Attraction
● **Waterford**

Below: glass factory, Waterford
Bottom: Georgian terrace in Waterford

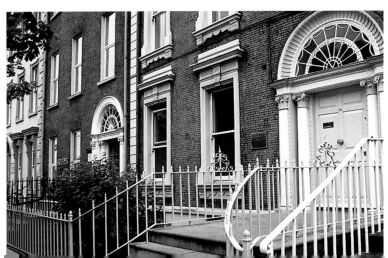

Map on page 46

John Roberts

While walking the streets of Waterford, one has to respect the productivity of the architect John Roberts (1714–1796). Two of the city's grandest cathedrals, Christ Church Cathedral and the Cathedral of the Most Holy Trinity, were designed by Roberts. In addition, he oversaw the building of many fine homes, one of which was the new Bishop's Palace. In return, the bishop gave Roberts the lease on the Old Bishop's Palace at No 1 and 2 Cathedral Square. This may seem a large house for an architect, but it was probably only just adequate for Roberts, his wife and 24 children.

Old townhouse in Youghal

WATERFORD CRYSTAL

Waterford is renowned throughout the world for its glassware. The modern **Waterford Crystal Factory** (guided tours Mar–Oct daily 8.30am–4pm; Nov–Feb Mon–Fri 9am–3.15pm), where glassblowers and engravers can be seen at work, is on the N25 to Cork, 1km (about a mile) from the town centre. The 18-minute audio-visual show explains the evolution of glassmaking, of course emphasising the role of Waterford since George and William Penros opened their factory in 1783, but the real excitement is visiting the factory floor where master craftsmen fashion molten glass then cut and polish each piece by hand. An extensive selection of crystal, both antique and modern, is on show, and there is a wide range of modern crystal for sale, including bargain 'seconds'.

TRAMORE

From Waterford, drive south to the coast at **Tramore**, the largest seaside resort in the area. The town itself looks rather shabby, with its amusement arcades and fish-and-chip shops, but the 5-km (3-mile) long sandy beach to the east, backed by high dunes, more than makes up for this. Continue westwards along the R675, through pretty villages, admiring the views en route. At **Bunmahon** it's best to turn left, in order to stay

as close as possible to the coast – the signpost to look out for is marked **Stradbally**. The beach here is particularly attractive, and the wooded cliffs all around are ideal for walks.

ALONG THE SEA INTO CORK

The next relatively large community is the market town and fishing harbour of **Dungarvan**, with good places to shop in and around Grattan Square.

To the south of Dungarvan, take the minor road nearest the coast. That way you'll see **Ardmore**, a small seaside town on the peninsula between Ardmore Bay and Youghal Bay. The 12th-century ruins of St Declan's Cathedral contain some carved Ogham stones. The 30-m (97-ft) high round tower beside it is in unusually good conditon.

★ **Youghal** (pronounced *Yawl*) is not by-passed by the main road, but is worth a visit for its long sandy beaches, historic buildings and seafood bar-restaurant *(see page 116, Aherne's)*. It was here that John Huston filmed the New Bedford sequences of *Moby Dick* in the early 1950s. The Clock Tower, a distinctive landmark built in 1776 as a jail, straddles the main road in the town centre. At the end of William Street is St Mary's Collegiate Church, Ireland's largest medieval church, built in the second half of the 15th century. Its oak roof and massive pulpit are interesting, as are the memorials to the English who conquered this part of Ireland.

At the beginning of August, Youghal plays host to the Premier International Busking Festival. These four nights of music, song, storytelling and street theatre attract artists from all over the world.

Another place to eat on this stretch of coast is **Ballymaloe House** in Shanagarry, one of the most famous hotels in southern Ireland *(see page 127)*. The nearby Ballymaloe Cookery School, run by Darina Allen, has a high reputation, and its kitchen and pleasure gardens are fun to visit (May–Sept daily 9am–6pm). There's probably no nicer place to eat in Ireland (that also goes for families with children). From here it is just half an hour's drive to Cork *(see page 54)*.

Sir Walter Raleigh
The Elizabethan adventurer was awarded substantial lands in Youghal for helping to suppress a rebellion in 1579. When he was warden of the town in 1588–59, he lived at Myrtle Grove, which can be seen from the precincts of St Mary's Collegiate Church, and it was here that he supposedly smoked the first pipe of tobacco and planted the first potatoes to be grown in Ireland.

Round tower at Ardmore

Map on page 56

Fota Arboretum

Fota Arboretum, on an island in Cork Harbour, contains an extensive collection of exotic plants, many native to the Southern Hemisphere. The gardens were laid out in the early 19th century. The arboretum and gardens can be reached by train from Cork or, by car, 14km (9 miles) along the Cobh Road. Open all year.

Cornmarket Street, Cork

4: Cork

Friendly, relaxing, hospitable: these are the adjectives applied to Cork. Yet within Ireland the inhabitants are often accused of being overly proud of their city, and of being permanently at odds with the 'arrogant' Dubliners. That may be a generalisation, but Cork does radiate a healthy self-confidence boosted by its highly successful year (2005) as European Capital of Culture. Many of the houses and churches in this busy harbour town were built from red sandstone in the late 18th and early 19th centuries. In contrast, their walls, portals or oriel windows are embellished with silvery-grey limestone, a style known locally as 'streaky bacon'.

The city centre lies on an island between two tributaries of the River Lee, and can be explored comfortably on foot.

HISTORY

The region around the delta of the River Lee has been densely inhabited since the Ice Age. A community grew up around a monastery founded by St Finbarr, the city's patron saint, on the south bank of the river in the 7th century. It was probably located on the site of today's cathedral. Old manuscripts mention that the monastery was attacked several times during the 9th century by Vikings, but by AD917 the Norsemen had settled down in the nearby marshland (the name 'Cork' is derived from the Old Irish *Corcaigh*, which means 'marshy place'), and were soon converted to Christianity.

The Anglo-Normans who arrived in 1177 drove out the Vikings and fortified the town. During the Middle Ages maritime trade grew in importance, and Cork had close ties with Bristol, Ypres and Bayonne. Wine, spices and other luxury goods were imported in exchange for furs, wool and linen. The political turmoil of the 17th century put an end to this trading; during the campaigns of Oliver Cromwell (1649) and William of Orange (1690), the city was occupied.

From the end of the 18th century a glass industry brought renewed prosperity. Cork experienced one of its darkest hours during the Anglo-Irish War of 1920–21 when it supported the republican cause. It was terrorised by the 'Black-and-Tans', the mercenaries in the pay of the British, and large parts of the city were burned. Traditional industries declined in the 1950s, but now pharmaceuticals, electronics and chemicals provide employment.

CITY TOUR

At the northern end of **St Patrick's Street**, the main shopping street in Cork, is one of the most well-known sights in the city: **'The Statue' ❶**. It depicts Father Theobald Matthew, a priest who preached abstinence and helped the poor during the 19th century.

St Patrick's Bridge ❷ leads over the North Channel of the River Lee. The steep hill straight ahead is St Patrick's Hill, and its attractive houses are worth a closer look. Then turn left and go up to ★ **St Anne's Church ❸**, which was built between 1722 and 1726. Its bell-tower is known as the 'Tower of Shandon' (open Mon–Sat 10am–5pm), notable not only for its unusual appearance (two almost white limestone walls and two of red sandstone), but also for the panoramic view from the top. Visitors are allowed and even encouraged to ring the famous bells.

Below: Bell of Shandon, Cork
Bottom: refurbished waterside apartments in Cork

Map
below

Opposite the church is the **Old Butter Exchange ❹**, which dates from the 18th century, when salted butter from Cork and Kerry was in demand all over Europe. Today it houses the Shandon Craft Centre.

St Finbarr's Cathedral, Cork

FITZGERALD PARK

On the south side of the North Channel, Fitzgerald Park contains the modest **Cork Public Museum ❺** (open Mon–Fri 11am–1pm and 2.15–5pm). Exhibitions document the city's more recent history, particularly the period 1916–23.

To the south of the museum is **University College ❻**. The north wing of the main building, erected in 1846, holds an important collection of Ogham stones, with runic script dating from the early days of the Celts and Picts (4th century AD). ★**Honan Chapel**, built in 1915, features some of the best examples of applied art dating from the 'Celtic Revival', including stained glass and mosaics. Don't miss the Lewis Glucksman Gallery, a striking modern building opened in 2004.

A short walk east, on the south bank of the South Channel, is ★ **St Finbarr's Cathedral ❼**. This astonishing neo-Gothic edifice was built in 1878. Some people find its colourful interior impressive, others can't wait to get out. Nearby, **Elizabeth**

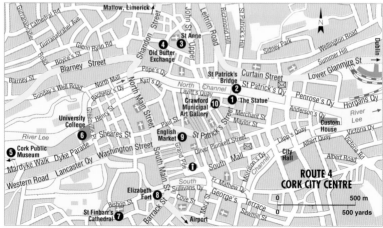

ROUTE 4
CORK CITY CENTRE

0   500 m
0   500 yards

Fort ❽ was built around 1600 and offers a good view from its battlements. If you cross Parliament Bridge you'll find yourself back in the city centre. Shoppers might like to take a look at Oliver Plunkett Street and Paul Street. Also, there is a flea market at the junction of Cornmarket and Coal Quay.

From St Patrick's Street, carry on to the **English Market** ❾ with its arrays of meat, fruit and vegetables. In Emmet Place, to the north of St Patrick's Street, is the **Cork Opera House**, dating from 1915.

Star Attraction
● Crawford Municipal Art Gallery

CRAWFORD MUNICIPAL ART GALLERY

Next to the Opera House is the ★★**Crawford Municipal Art Gallery** ❿ (open Mon–Fri 10am–5pm, Sat 9am–1pm). The impressive facade of the former Custom House (1724) is integrated into a red brick extension by Eric van Egeraat, completed in 2001. This is used for touring exhibitions; the collection concentrates on Irish art from the 18th century to the present day. Alongside 18th-century silver and glass are paintings by James Barry and Jack B. Yeats, and stained glass by Harry Clarke.

Gallery café
Don't leave the Crawford Municipal Art Gallery without first treating yourself to coffee and cake or more in the Crawford Gallery Café – possibly the best museum restaurant café between London and New York. It is a branch of the renowned Ballymaloe House at Shanagarry *(see page 53).*

EXCURSION FROM CORK

Anyone keen on seeing the lush green landscape of County Cork should take a brief tour west of the city along the R618, as far as **Macroom**. This pretty town with its Tuesday market lies in the midst of some splendid scenery. Despite the idyllic atmosphere in this region, the signs of historical conflict are never far away. Along the R585 south of Macroom there are signposts near Bealnablath to 'Site of Ambush'.

This is where Michael Collins, the main resistance leader in the war for independence against the British, was shot dead on 22 August 1922 by republicans who saw him as a traitor to their cause. Against his own political convictions, and in the interests of peace, he had taken part in the Anglo-Irish negotiations that led to the partition of the island. As he signed the treaty he said: 'Early this morning I signed my death warrant.' Eight months later his prediction came true.

Irish knitwear attracts tourist dollars

Map on facing page

A taste of Kinsale

Kinsale is renowned as the gastronomic capital of Ireland: 12 of its highly-acclaimed restaurants have combined to form the 'Good Food Circle'. They organise an annual Autumn Flavours in October (to find out more, contact the tourist information office).

5: The Southwest

Kinsale – Castletownshend – Baltimore – Bantry – Beara Peninsula – Kenmare – Ring of Kerry – Killarney – Dingle – Tralee – Limerick (approx 600km/370 miles)

The counties of Cork and Kerry, with their varied peninsulas jutting out into the Atlantic Ocean, are the most often visited regions of Ireland outside of Dublin. This route starts south of Cork and follows the coast to Skibbereen, then turns north to Bantry, taking in the dramatic scenery of the Beara, Kerry and Dingle peninsulas and the rocky offshore islands. The thought of travelling around one rocky promontory after another might seem rather unappealing, but for many people rounding the next headland – from Mizen Head, Sheep's Head, Cod's Head, Lamb's Head and Slea Head to Loop Head – is addictive. They keep coming back for more.

Kinsale harbour

KINSALE

The colourful town of ★ **Kinsale**, the starting point of this route, is noted for its charming 18th-century houses. It was an important naval base from the 17th to the 19th centuries with its own shipyards and barracks. The scale of its importance can be judged from the size of ★ **Charles Fort** (open mid-Mar–Oct daily 10am–6pm; Nov–mid-Mar Sat–Sun 10am–5pm), which guards the harbour entrance. This enormous star-shaped 17th-century fortress is one of the best-preserved structures of its kind in Europe. A pleasant 3-km (2-mile) footpath leads from the town centre to the fort – just follow the 'Scilly Walk' signs. (Monty Python fans are advised not to take this too literally: Scilly is the part of the town on the eastern side of the bay.)

The former law courts building in the market square contains an excellent local history museum. A momentous date in Kinsale's history is 1601, when Spanish ships arrived to help the Irish princes in their struggle against the English. The Spanish and Irish were heavily defeated by Elizabeth I's troops at the Battle of Kinsale.

OLD HEAD OF KINSALE

Continue along the coast in a southwesterly direction. To discover the best beaches and cliffs it's always worth turning off the main road. One particularly worthwhile detour is to the ★ **Old Head of Kinsale**, a promontory with a fine view across Courtmacsherry Bay. The next large town is **Clonakilty**, a popular tourist resort within easy reach of Inchedoney and several other broad sandy beaches.

Map on page 59

Clear Island
From Baltimore, the journey out to Clear Island is particularly popular. It is the southernmost point of Ireland, excluding the Fastnet Rock 6km (4 miles) to the west. Clear Island has a Gaelic-speaking population of around 100. It also has a seabird research station. Every morning in July and August, enormous flocks of stormy petrels leave their nesting places on the mainland coast and pass Clear Island as they head out to sea. They return in the evening, skimming just above the ocean surface.

The route to Skibbereen passes through several coastal villages, starting with **Rosscarbery**. From here it's best to turn off the N71 again on to the winding R597 coast road, past the prehistoric **stone circle of Drombeg** and on to **Glandore**. William Thompson, a noted eccentric, was born in Rosscarbery in 1785. He was a landowner who turned his estates into a co-operative for the 700 or so people living there. He was also an atheist, a vegetarian, a social theorist (one of his books was quoted by Karl Marx in volume I of *Das Kapital*) and a fervent advocate of women's rights. Not so eccentric after all, by modern standards.

CASTLETOWNSHEND

The most attractive village along this part of the coast is ★ **Castletownshend**, with its magnificent main street sloping steeply down towards the harbour. It's appearance suggests that Castletownshend was a prosperous Anglo-Irish community in the not-too-distant past. Indeed, it was here that the village's two most celebrated authors worked in the early 20th century. Using the pseudonyms of 'Somerville and Ross', Edith Somerville and her cousin Violet Martin wrote humorous descriptions of the Anglo-Irish upper class's attempts to come to terms with the shifting power relationships. Their whimsical depictions of resident mag-

The stone circle of Drombeg

istrates and cunning locals in such works as *Some Experiences of an Irish R.M.* are still popular.

BALTIMORE

From Castletownshend the road leads to **Skibereen**, a market town with plenty of good shops (the market is held every Wednesday). It's often said that this town owes its existence to Algerian pirates – and it is true that several terrified members of the coastal population moved inland and settled here after a North African pirate ship attacked the harbour of ★ **Baltimore** and forcibly enslaved around 200 people. Baltimore is a far more peaceful place these days, apart from the tourists who go there for the superb view of the Atlantic coast, and to take boat trips out to Cape Clear Island (45 minutes) and Sherkin Island (10 minutes).

Below: Lough Ine, Skibbereen
Bottom: local crafts on show at Schull

MIZEN HEAD

To the northwest of Skibbereen, one majestic promontory follows another, like the fingers of a giant hand stretching out into the Atlantic. In Ballydehob, turn off the N71 to reach the small village of **Schull** (marked as 'Skull' on some maps), situated on the 'first finger'. The busy yachting harbour with its arts and crafts shops lies at the foot of the 400-m (1,300-ft) high Mount Gabriel; the two gigantic white domes of the radar station at the top look rather incongruous.

At the end of the peninsula is Barley Cove, which contains the very best beach for far and wide. Continue on to ★ **Mizen Head**, the southernmost point on the Irish mainland, where the former lighthouse keeper's quarters are now a stunning visitor centre (open daily mid-Mar–May and Oct 10.30am–5pm, June–Sept 10am–6pm) on a rocky island reached by an arched footbridge.

BANTRY

The market town and fishing harbour of **Bantry** is an ideal base for discovering Ireland's southwest peninsulas.

Map on page 59

Below and bottom:
Bantry House

On the first Friday in every month, a general market is held in the main square. Several people who moved here from Britain and the Continent (nicknamed 'blow-ins' by the locals) can be seen peddling their wares of wholefoods, arts and crafts. The statue in the square is of St Brendan the Navigator. Legend has it that St Brendan began his epic sea journey here, and discovered America between AD535 and 553.

★ **Bantry House** (open daily 9am–6pm; often until 8pm in summer) is a country estate in a magnificent setting just outside the town. Built between 1700 and 1710, it was greatly extended around 1840. Trees were cleared to create a large lawn, affording fine views of Bantry Bay, Whiddy Island and the violet-brown hills of the Beara Peninsula.

The house contains a fine collection of treasures, including 18th-century French and Irish furniture, Aubusson carpets and Gobelin tapestries. For ten days in late June/early July, Bantry House hosts the West Cork Chamber Music Festival, which attracts a fine line-up of international musicians to this idyllic setting.

BEARA PENINSULA

The main road from Bantry to Kenmare (N71) is quite a scenic route, especially from the top

of the pass. Nevertheless, for anyone with time on their hands it's worth setting off from Glengariff on the 110-km (68-mile) trip around the ★★**Beara Peninsula**. The Caha Mountains run along the middle of the peninsula, giving the south coast a particularly mild climate. Travel west on the R572 and you'll pass beneath the rocky wall of Hungry Hill, which, including its waterfall, is 684m (2,200ft) above sea level.

The region lying to the west and the north of **Castletownbere** (officially Castletown Bearhaven), with Bear Island just off the coast, is one of the most attractive in Ireland. The landscape has been altered by deforestation and dairy farming, and ruined castles alternate with disused copper mines (near Allihies). The coastline here is considerably more impressive than anything on the two peninsulas to the north, though they are more popular with tourists.

Star Attractions
● Beara Peninsula
● Iveragh

Sheep's Head Peninsula
To the southwest of Bantry is Sheep's Head, the narrowest and least developed of the peninsulas. For good views across Bantry Bay, follow the 'Goat's Path Scenic Route', which leads up to the point beside Sheep's Head.

RING OF KERRY

Kenmare, with its pastel-coloured houses, is the usual starting-point for the Ring of Kerry round trip. The small town, founded by a handful of Englishmen in 1670, has every tourist convenience imaginable, including two of the most luxurious hotels in Ireland, both of which have been awarded the much-coveted Michelin star (only six hotels in the Republic have been accorded the honour): the Park Hotel and Sheen Falls Lodge (*see Accommodation, page 126*). This is also a convenient base for anglers.

A trip round the peninsula of ★★**Iveragh** must not be missed; it has some of the most magnificent landscape in Europe, as any of the hundreds of people on bicycles, motorbikes, cars and buses travelling the 180-km (110-mile) long coast road will tell you. Starting the Ring of Kerry trip from Kenmare has the advantage that you'll meet the countless buses from Killarney coming the other way, instead of being stuck behind them. One way to avoid the crush is to turn off down the minor roads to some fine beaches, such as those near Parknasilla, Derrynane or Glenbeigh.

The Beara Peninsula

Map
on page
59

Killarney Pony Cab
Anyone eager to see the sights from a pony and trap can hire one of the many 'jaunting cars' for a round trip of Killarney, together with cheerful explanations from the driver.

ISLANDS OR MOUNTAINS

From Waterville or Portmagee boat trips operate to the Skellig Islands and the 1,200-year-old monastery of ★★ **Skellig Michael**, described by George Bernard Shaw as being more like a dream than reality. The monks who lived here until the 12th century were accommodated in strange round huts with small holes in the roof; it is hard to imagine a more isolated existence.

Another option is to head inland to the mountain range known as **MacGillicuddy's Reeks**. Those who manage to find their way to Lough Acoose beneath Carrauntoohil Peak (1,041m/ 3,415ft) should leave their car and – with the right equipment and a good map – take the hiking route known as the Coomloughra Horseshoe along the ridge between Caher, Carrantuohill and Beenkeragh. It not only scales the highest mountain in Ireland but also provides great views.

AROUND KILLARNEY

The town of **Killarney** itself is rural and pleasant, but subservient to tourism. It has more hotels than any other Irish town, Dublin excepted, yet still retains its charm. It is worth 'doing' Killarney for the beauty of its lakes and vegetation. The best introduction is an organised, day-long Gap of Dunloe tour – a minibus to the Gap, a pony and

Riding through the Gap of Dunloe, Killarney

trap ride or a walk through the Gap, and a boat trip back to Ross Castle. Book through Killarney Tourist Office, tel: 064-31633, www.corkkerry.ie.

The vicinity has much to offer. **Inisfallen**, the largest of Lough Leane', has the ruins of a medieval monastery and is reached by boat from **Ross Castle**.

Killarney National Park is around 10,000 hectares (24,700 acres) in size. At its centre is the magnificent **Muckross House** (open Nov–mid-Mar 9am–5.30pm; mid-Mar–June and Sept–Oct until 6pm; July–Aug until 7pm), built in 1843 in Elizabethan style. The house contains the **Kerry Folklife Centre**, which shows how the local rural population lived in past centuries.

DINGLE PENINSULA

The ★★★ **Dingle Peninsula** is magnificent. In Castlemaine, turn off the N70 on to the R561 and take the road as far as **Inch**. The western side of the narrow promontory to the south of the village is taken up by a wonderful 5-km (3-mile) long sandy beach. In summer it's difficult to resist taking off your shoes and going for a seaside stroll. At sunset the view along the coast and across the sea to the Blasket Islands is truly breathtaking.

Dingle is a busy fishing village-cum-holiday resort, with pubs, bed-and-breakfasts and restaurants lining its harbour promenade. For a restful night's sleep, stay away from the busy waterside.

From Dingle, the R559 goes round Slea Head – the next piece of mainland to the west of here is the Canadian coast of Labrador. Just before Slea Head the road passes **Ventry**, which has a beautiful sheltered beach. About 6km (4 miles) southwest of the village a country track is signposted to the ruins of **Dunbeg Fort**, an amazingly complex Iron Age fortress overlooking the sea.

BALLYFERRITER

In the high street in **Ballyferriter** there is a Heritage Centre (open June–Sept daily 11am–6pm), providing information on recent local history as well as the innumerable prehistoric and

Star Attractions
- **Skellig Michael**
- **Dingle Peninsula**

Below: Slea Head, on the Dingle Peninsula
Below: enjoying a pint in O'Flaherty's pub in Dingle

Map on page 59

Blasket Island

The threatening-looking Blasket Islands, rising 300m (1,000ft) above the sea, are visible offshore from the Dingle and Kerry coastlines. Until 1953 a community of Gaelic-speaking fishermen and farmers inhabited the Blaskets. The western part of the Dingle Peninsula is considered *Gaeltacht (see page 12)* and many of the residents still speak a form of Gaelic. Boat excursions to the Blasket Islands depart from Dunquin and Dingle.

Early Christian finds from the region, such as the remains of the 5th-century monastery of Riasc. The monastery was discovered around half a mile from the village and contained an ornamental stone that is considered to be the forerunner of the Celtic high cross.

The most magnificent Early Christian monument is the ★ **Gallarus Oratory** to the east of Ballyferriter. This small chapel has stood here for 1,200 years and is a model of elegant simplicity and aesthetic perfection. Its waterproof construction of flat stone without the use of mortar has survived the test of time. From Gallarus the road winds its way back to Dingle.

From Dingle, take the road leading northwards across the ★ **Connor Pass**. At the top (457m/1,500ft above sea-level) is the most beautiful view of the peninsula imaginable. It takes in the awe-inspiring Mount Brandon and the broad sweep of Brandon Bay. The latter is bounded to the east by a promontory and contains Ireland's longest sandy beach, **Stradbally Strand**, which continues for an uninterrupted sweep of 18km (11 miles).

Below: the Gallarus Oratory
Bottom: feeding swans in Limerick

TRALEE AND LIMERICK

Tralee, the regional centre of Kerry, is perhaps less inviting than the more visitor-oriented Killarney. In August it takes on a party atmosphere for the annual Rose of Tralee Festival, a beauty and personality pageant.

From here, head inland to **Limerick**, the third-largest city in the Republic (pop. 75,000), with its **Hunt Museum** (Custom House, Charlotte's Quay, open Tues–Sat 10am–5pm, Sun 2–5pm), which contains a superb collection of early Celtic and medieval art. The old, chiefly Georgian, part of town lies to the north of Arthur's Quay. The Tourist Information Office on Arthur's Quay is the starting point for walking tours following the sites described in Frank McCourt's memoir, *Angela's Ashes*. For the best views, climb one of the round towers of the 13th-century **King John's Castle** (open mid-Apr–Oct 9.30am–5.30pm; Nov–mid-Apr Sun noon–4pm).

6: The West

Ennis – Lisdoonvarna – Galway – Clifden – Westport – Achill Island – Ballina – Sligo (approx 450km/290 miles)

Map on page 68

Everything that conquerors before the 17th century found so uninteresting about the west of Ireland is the main reason why visitors come here today. The thinly populated, barren stretches of landscape with serrated coastlines, especially in Connaught to the west of loughs Corrib, Mask and Conn, have a magnetic appeal.

EMIGRATION

The region is usually referred to as 'unspoilt', but in the context of Irish history that means 'poor'. The truth is that the terrain in the west of Ireland is unsuitable for dairy farming. The Great Famine of 1845–51 claimed more victims in Connaught than anywhere else in the country and the Gaelic-speaking population of Connemara and Mayo has been considered 'backward' by more progressive Irish people for a long time. The area to the west of the Shannon had the smallest proportion of Anglo-Irish Protestants, and hence investments, before 1922. No wonder that the west has such a long tradition of emigration, even if 'only' to

Below: traditional life survives in the West
Bottom: Poulnabrone Dolmen in the Burren (see page 71)

Map below

Dublin (a 1926 census registered that Connaught had just one-third of its 1841 population, while Dublin's population had almost doubled in the same period).

Although statistics show that things have improved since the 1970s thanks to tourism, new industry and European Union subsidies, this region is still the poorest in Ireland. Anyone who visits the *Gaeltacht* (Gaelic-speaking areas) in the west of Galway, the northwest of Mayo and the Aran Islands, and marvels at the scenery and the traditions, should remember what it has cost the population to remain true to their homeland.

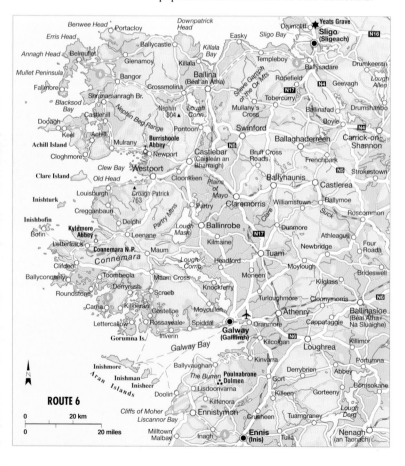

CLIFFS OF MOHER

The capital of Clare is **Ennis**, which is a good base for exploring the county, from the steep coastline near Kilkee and Moher to the limestone carst landscape of the Burren.

From Ennis, the main road (N85) leads to the delightful town of **Ennistymon**, and from there via Lahinch and its popular surfing beach to Hag's Head, the southern end of the ★★ **Cliffs of Moher**. This 8-km (5-mile) long stretch of vertical cliffs, which rises to 203m (660ft) high, is spectacular. Near the northern end of the cliffs there is a visitors' centre (open June–Aug 9am–8pm; Sept–May 9.30am–5.30pm) with a large car park, a café, a souvenir shop and an observation platform.

Star Attraction
● Cliffs of Moher

Across Liscannor Bay
On reaching the end of the road at Hag's Head on the Cliffs of Moher, those with the time and the inclination to continue on foot for around an hour will be rewarded with a superb view not only northwards along the cliffs but also far to the south, across Liscannor Bay and Mal Bay.

DOOLIN

Follow the coast road northwards as far **Doolin**, which is reputed to have the best traditional music for miles around in its pubs and bars. The village seems to extend for ever along its main street, and there's a simple reason for it: today's Doolin is a combination of two villages, Fisherstreet and Roadford, known as 'Lower Village' and 'Upper Village'. The place made its name in the 1960s when a series of musicians, most of them named Russell and related to one another, performed here in O'Connor's Pub. There has been a steady stream of visitors ever since, and each pub holds regular sessions (others include McGann's and McDermotts in Roadford).

Many of the people visit Doolin aren't necessarily interested in rest and relaxation, and several unpleasant exchanges with local farmers have led to camping being forbidden in the area. There is a campsite at the harbour, not far from where the ferries leave for the Aran Islands *(see page 73)* in the summer.

O'Brien's Tower on the Cliffs of Moher

LISDOONVARNA

Inland from the Cliffs of Moher, the town of **Lisdoonvarna** has, since the early 19th century, earned a reputation as a health resort because of

Map on page 68

Below: waterfall at Ailwee Caves, Ballyvaughan
Bottom: The Burren landscape

its sulphur springs. The place still has the air of a late 19th-century town. Most visitors who stop here on their way from the Cliffs of Moher to Galway go to the **Spa Wells Centre** (open June–Oct daily 10am–6pm) in the middle of the park to bathe in the sulphur spring water. The water is said to have various beneficial effects, particularly for curing rheumatic ailments.

THE BURREN

Lisdoonvarna is surrounded to the north and east by the remarkable carst landscape known as **★★ The Burren**. This region of porous limestone, with its bare rocky hills full of caves, covers an area of 260sq km (100sq miles). The rock has been eroded by glaciation, and moraines have left erratic blocks literally strewn about. It was only fierce protests during the 1980s that prevented speculators from actually clearing away the rocks and exporting them to Britain as decorations for 'Oriental' gardens. During prehistoric times this landscape was covered with a thin layer of earth and vegetation, but around 5,000 years ago the first settlers arrived and began to clear the land and graze their animals. The resulting erosion eventually stripped the rock bare.

Despite its sparse appearance this area is the most botanically interesting in Europe. It contains

1,100 of the 1,200 different species of plant native to Ireland. The fauna is just as varied: wild goats, Irish hares, foxes and badgers all live here, as do ermine (especially the 'small but nasty' variety known as *Mustela erminea hibernica*).

For a closer look, put on sturdy shoes and, armed with a map, set off from **Ballinalacken Castle** northwest of Lisdoonvarna along the 'Burren Way', heading north towards Ballyvaughan. The signposted route is 40km (24 miles) long and begins further south in Liscannor, but this section leads through the rockiest part of the Burren and is only about half as long.

THE LEGACY OF THE BURREN

The Burren (*boireann* means rocky place in Irish) may appear a little desolate, but it is steeped in history. To date, more than 60 megalithic tombs and no fewer than 500 Stone Age circles have been discovered in the region. The most striking megalith is ★ **Poulnabrone Dolmen** on the R480, a table-shaped stone tomb originally covered with earth, dating from around 3000BC *(see photograph, page 67)*. The massive slab on top measures more than 2m (6ft) by 3m (10ft).

The magnificent stone fort of ★ **Cahercommaun**, situated in a dramatic position above a river valley, dates from the 8th century AD. An unnumbered road leads from the R480 to the village of Carran, where you can park your car and follow the signposted route up to the fort.

In **Kilfenora**, on the southern edge of the Burren, is the **Burren Display Centre** (open Mar–May and Oct daily 10am–5pm; June–Sept 9.30am–6pm), which contains exhibitions and displays documenting the local geology, archaeology, flora and fauna.

GALWAY

For many people ★★ **Galway**, the capital of the county of the same name and Ireland's fourth largest city, is the way they always imagined Ireland to be. The houses at the harbour and in the

Star Attractions
● **The Burren**
● **Galway**

The useless Burren
Oliver Cromwell's General Ludlow reputedly said of the Burren: 'Not enough wood to hang a man, not enough water to drown him, not enough clay to cover his corpse.'

Lahinch Bay, a sandy beach near The Burren

Maps
on pages
68 & 74

Oyster Fever

The start of the oyster season at the beginning of September is marked by the Oyster Festival at the traditional mussel harbour of Clarinbridge, just south of Galway. Activities include oyster-opening and oyster-eating competitions, music and drinking. At the end of the month, the procedure is repeated with even more enthusiasm and abandon in Galway with four days of dancing and celebrations. Cynics reckon that the only reason the people of Galway eat so many oysters in such a short space of time at the beginning of the season is because most are exported – 80 percent of the catch goes abroad, mostly to Germany and Switzerland.

Galway's Clarenbridge Oyster Festival is held in September

old town date back to the 16th century, and many are still in remarkably good condition. University College, Galway, was founded in 1849 and has an excellent reputation. A number of its students are from the Continent and North America.

The surrounding area is just what every fan of Ireland is looking for: the Burren is only a few miles south of the city; **Lough Corrib** (the largest lough in the Republic) is to the north, surrounded by lush green meadows and pastureland divided by stone walls; Connemara and the Aran Islands *(see opposite)* are to the west, with their wild and romantic coasts; and the *Gaeltacht* contributes to Galway's flourishing role as a centre of the study of Gaelic. Restaurants here also serve the famous oysters from Galway Bay.

GALWAY CITY TOUR

The best place to start a tour of Galway is **Eyre Square**. The green part of the square with all the monuments is officially known as John F. Kennedy Memorial Park. To the south is the Eyre Square Shopping Centre, containing signs directing pedestrians to Medieval Street – so named because a section of the ancient town wall has been preserved at the centre of the modern shops. At the end of the wall go out into William Street, which – together with the extensions of Shop Street, High Street and Quay Street – leads through the medieval centre of Galway past a series of interesting emporiums. Powell's, for example, is a great place to buy Irish music and instruments. There is also Eason's Bookshop, Kenny's Bookshop and Gallery, and a number of arts and crafts centres. Despite the attractions of the partly wooden shopfronts, keep your eyes on the top sections of the buildings, because the coats-of-arms and inscriptions on their brickwork illustrate just how old they are.

Quay Street ends at Wolfe Tone Bridge, where the Corrib river flows out into Galway Bay creating harbour basins on either side. Turn left at the river and soon a 16th-century structure known as the Spanish Arch comes into view. This was so named because Spanish ships are reputed to have unloaded their wine barrels here at that time.

On the other side of the city, beside the river, is the Catholic episcopal **Cathedral of Our Lady Assumed into Heaven and St Nicholas**, begun in 1957 and completed in 1965. This 300-ft (91-m) long building is a strange mixture of styles and ornaments, a hodge-podge of Romanesque arches, Tudor rosettes and a Renaissance dome. The resident bishop of Galway at the time was Dr Eamonn Casey, a fierce opponent of birth control and contraception. He made international news in 1992 when it transpired that his former mistress was living in the USA with her 18-year-old son at the church's expense. The bishop swiftly resigned and went to South America to work as a missionary.

ARAN ISLANDS

The ★★★ **Aran Islands** lie off the mouth of Galway Bay rather like a barrier. Geologically they are a continuation of the limestone massif of the Burren and the landscape appears to consist only of stone with little tufts of green. Prehistoric and Early Christian remains can be found here, along with several stone cottages, some of them built as recently as the beginning of the 20th century.

The three inhabited islands of Inishmore ('large island'), Inishmaan ('middle island') and Inisheer

Star Attraction
● Aran Islands

Below: Galway City
Bottom: traditional transport on the Aran Islands

The Walls of Aran
The stone walls winding over the landscape, which divide up the fields and pastureland, are one of the distinctive features of the Aran Islands. There appears to be no rhyme or reason to them; sometimes they just encircle expanses of bare rock.

Dún Aengus coastal fort

('eastern island') cover 4,450 hectares (11,000 acres) and have a population of around 1,450, all of whom have Gaelic as their mother tongue.

The islands can be reached by plane from Inverin on the Connemara coast, or by ferry. Several rival ferry companies operate from Galway City (the longest crossing at 3 hours), Doolin in Clare (about 40 minutes), and Rossaveale in Connemara (usually the cheapest at an hour). Boats also ply between the various islands but the boat operators are fiercely competitive, and tickets are not transferable. Confirm the timetable with the skipper. There's no need for a car on the Aran Islands; even Inishmore, where there are bicycle or pony and trap hire and public minibuses, is only 13km (8 miles) long and nowhere wider than 2km (1 mile).

INISHMORE

Bus excursions with communicative drivers take visitors from Kilronan harbour on Inishmore to the sights of the island, the most spectacular of which is ★★ **Dún Aengus**, a massive stone fortress on cliffs 90m (300ft) above the sea. On the landward side, three successive walls, each up to 5m (15ft) in height, form an impressive semicircular ruin. Who exactly built the fortress and when is unclear. Estimates range from 500BC to the 8th century AD. Legends mention the once-powerful tribe of the Fir Bolg, who sought refuge here from the Celts. Other stone forts, megalithic tombs and Early Christian structures are dotted across all three islands.

North Sound
★Rossaveel
Galway
Inis Mór
(Inishmore)
Cill Mhuirbhigh
(Killmurvy)
Onaght
Oghil
Dun
Aengus
Cill Rónáin
(Kilronan)
Inis Meáin
(Inishmaan)
Killeany
Galway
Inishmaan
Dun Conor
**OILEÁIN ARAINN
(ARAN ISLANDS)**
0   10 km
Doolin
Inis Oirr
(Inisheer)

CONNEMARA

★★ **Connemara** is the official name of the *Gaeltacht* (Gaelic-speaking) section of County Galway on the peninsula to the west of loughs Corrib and Mask. The region is bordered to the south by Galway Bay and to the north by the narrow bay known as Killary Harbour. Today, it usually includes the region to the north as far as Clew Bay and Westport. The name Connemara is an abbreviation of the Irish *Conmaicne-Mara*, which translates to 'tribe of the Conmac by the sea'. According to legend, the region was given by Queen Maev to one of her sons.

Since there are several rewarding ways of getting from Galway to Clifden, the 'capital of Connemara' and the largest town in the region, it's worth taking detours from whichever route you opt for. The N59 is the quickest connection from Galway to Clifden. It leads through the magnificent interior, past innumerable tiny lakes, the Maamturk Mountains and, in the north, the Twelve Bens (marked on some maps as the Twelve Pins).

The other option is to travel along the northern edge of Galway Bay and then, just past Inverin, to plunge into the confusion of narrow side-roads and get lost for a few hours (or a few days) among all those tracks that run across bridges to islands off the coast, or to the ends of promontories.

CLIFDEN

Along this stretch of coast, the houses become more prosperous-looking the further west you travel (and also look as if they're only inhabited during holiday season, too). In **Cashel Bay** there are several Victorian country houses, such as

Star Attractions
● **Dún Aengus**
● **Connemara**

Below: Connemara's dramatic landscape
Bottom: the coast between Roundstone and Clifden

Map on page 68

Excursion from Clifden
There's a good excursion from Clifden, signposted from the marketplace as 'Sky Road'. It leads 13km (8 miles) in a long arc across to a promontory in the west, with a superb view of the Atlantic coast and of Clifden as well.

Cashel House *(see page 124)*, which were originally built as 'sporting lodges' – i.e. for hunting and fishing – and now serve as hotels. It's clear from looking at **Clifden** how popular the western part of Connemara was with the Anglo-Irish upper classes in the 19th century. This town, founded in 1812 on the land of local squire John D'Arcy, contrasts with the long 'street villages' of the region in that it has its own marketplace, from which the other main streets radiate. Today, Clifden is a tourist centre complete with shops, pubs and restaurants.

CONNEMARA NATIONAL PARK

One of the oldest and most attractive nature reserves in Ireland is the ★★**Connemara National Park**, which extends northeast from Clifden across 2,000 hectares (5,000 acres) of peat bog, rock and heather. The visitors' centre is in the village of Letterfrack (open Apr, May and Sept daily 10am–5.30pm; June–Aug 9.30am–6.30pm; nature trail; 2–3hr guided hikes July–Aug).

East of Letterfrack, the imposing **Kylemore Abbey** can be seen off to the left of the main road (N59). This neo-Gothic structure, built in 1866 as a country seat for the merchant and politician Mitchell Henry, has been a Benedictine convent and exclusive girls' boarding school since 1922.

Kylemore Abbey, a much photographed mansion

Parts of the abbey and its grounds are open to visitors during the summer (9am–5.30pm).

CLARE ISLAND

The shore of the bay known as Killary Harbour marks the border separating the counties of Galway and Mayo. From here, the R335 leads through a wild and romantic valley containing the 'black lake' of Doo Lough, and then on to the pretty village of **Louisburgh** with its 18th-century houses. There are several extensive (and mostly empty) sandy beaches in the area, such as Old Head, Berta Strand and Carrowniskey Strand, all of them providing good views of ★ **Clare Island** in Clew Bay. Boat trips to the island are available from Roonah Quay, west of the village (the journey takes around 25 minutes; tel: 098-25212 for ferry information).

Today, around 140 people live on this 2,000-hectare (4,950-acre) island; before the famine of 1845–51 the population was 1,700. Surrounding the decayed remains of the community's old cottages, the bare green fields reveal the distinctive outlines of former potato fields. The plants were placed in a slightly raised position so that rainwater could drain off, preventing mildew.

The fortress tower at the harbour was once part of the headquarters of the infamous pirate queen Granuaile, otherwise known as Grace O'Malley, who terrorised the coast during the 16th century and had bases on several islands. Her infamous story can be read in the **Granuaile Visitor Centre** in Louisburgh (open June–Sept Mon–Sat 10am–7.30pm). Adjacent to the centre is a small Famine Exhibition.

CROAGH PATRICK

Returning to the mainland, east of Louisburgh the road leads along the southern edge of Clew Bay. On the right, Ireland's famous pilgrimage mountain of **Croagh Patrick** soon comes into view. It is climbed by pilgrims all year round, though most of the 60,000 believers who come here

Star Attraction
● Connemara National Park

Below: Clare Island
Bottom: Grace O'Malley Fort

Map on page 68

Famine Museum
For a detailed description of the Great Famine visit the award-winning Famine Museum in Strokestown, south of Carrick-on-Shannon in County Roscommon (open Easter–Oct 11am–5.30pm).

Below: Westport House
Bottom: Westport in summer

arrive on the Sunday before 1 August. St Patrick is said to have fasted on this mountain for 40 days before defeating the pagan deity Crom. From the peak he is reputed to have rung his bell and banished all reptiles from Ireland – which is why there are no snakes anywhere in the country.

WESTPORT

The town of ★ **Westport** was the vision of local landowner John Browne (1709–76) who devised a scheme to move the existing village in order to extend the parkland around his manor house. The new town was planned and laid out in the late 18th century by the leading architect of the time, James Wyatt. Wyatt had the River Carrowbeg partially turned into a waterway and it now functions as the 'central strip' of the picturesqe Mall. Around Bridge Street and the Octagon there are numerous shops, pubs and cafés.

Browne's manor, **Westport House** (open May and Sept daily 2–5pm; June 2–6pm; July–Aug Mon–Sat 10.30am–6pm, Sun 2–6pm), built in 1730 by the German architect Richard Cassels and completed by Wyatt, occupies a glorious setting overlooking Clew Bay. It has several elegantly decorated and furnished rooms. The grounds accommodate a variety of attractions, including a children's animal and bird park and a flume ride.

ACHILL ISLAND

From Westport, continue northwards along the bay. Beyond **Newport**, a reputable angling centre, look out for the signpost on the left to **Burrishoole Abbey**. This ruined Dominican abbey, founded in 1486, is romantically situated on the shore of Newport Bay.

Achill Island is so remote that people have been steadily abandoning it since the 19th century. A few years ago, however, summer visitors began to arrive, mainly from Dublin, and have since been gradually converting the houses into holiday homes and building clusters of new ones. The largest island off the west coast of Ireland, connected with the mainland via a bridge, Achill is worth a visit for the views, the mountain landscape, and also the several fine, clean beaches (especially near Keel, Keem and Doagh).

THE MULLET

Erris in northwestern Mayo is one of the loneliest and windiest parts of Ireland, but fans of the Atlantic coast shouldn't miss it. The village of **Belmullet**, on the neck of land leading out to the hammer-shaped peninsula known as **The Mullet**, is refreshingly free from any signs of tourism. Empty flat beaches are a feature here. The biggest event is the annual August fair when emigrants return home from all over the world.

North of the Mullet, a sight worth seeing is the dramatic rocky coastline at **Benwee Head**. To reach it, turn off the R314 at Glenamoy. The road inland to **Ballina** crosses seemingly interminable peat bogs. Ballina (pop. 6,500) is the largest town in County Mayo and a popular angling centre (salmon in the Moy river, trout in Lough Conn).

SLIGO

East of Ballina, the route leaves Mayo and, following the coast, arrives at ★ **Sligo**, capital of the county of the same name and a major centre for

Below: Sligo Abbey
Bottom: Achill Island

Map
on page
68

W.B. Yeats statue, Sligo

William Butler Yeats
Despite his Protestant background, Yeats (1865–1939) had a profound love for the ancient rituals and pagan beliefs of Catholic Ireland, and his unwavering support for independence led to him becoming a senator in the Free State's first government. His unrequited love for the beautiful Irish patriot Maud Gonne, who acted in some of his plays, inspired much of his work. He was awarded the Nobel Prize for Literature in 1923.

the surrounding region. The small-town atmosphere here is refreshing, and life is hardly ever hectic; things only become somewhat strained during peak season in the summer. That's when the streets fill with thousands of tourists, many of them on the trail of William Butler Yeats.

The celebrated poet, dramatist and Irish nationalist politician spent the good part of his childhood here in his mother's native town, and kept coming back to visit Sligo later in life. He died in France in 1939 and was buried there because of the outbreak of World War II. After the war, in 1948, the body was finally taken back to Sligo and reinterred. Now, in accordance with his wishes, he lies in a little Protestant churchyard in Drumcliff, to the north of the town, at the foot of the mountain known as Ben Bulben. The epitaph 'Cast a cold eye On life, on death. Horseman, pass by!' comes from Yeats's own poem *Under Ben Bulben*.

HOMAGE TO YEATS

Yeats's enthusiasm for fast-vanishing aristocratic values, the humanism, courtesy and civility of the Italian Renaissance, the wisdom of ancient China, esoteric movements such as theosophy, and arts that enabled their audience to pass for a few moments into what he called 'a deep of the mind that had hitherto been too subtle for our habitation' have made this aesthetic genius one of Ireland's most popular literary figures.

The **Model Arts and Niland Gallery** (Tues–Sat 10am–5.30pm) in The Mall, a cleverly converted 19th-century school, is a multi-purpose arts centre. The gallery houses a major collection of works by Jack B. Yeats, who loved to paint his childhood haunts in Sligo and Rosses Point.

The **Sligo County Museum and Library** (open Tues–Fri 10am–5pm, Sat 10am–1pm and 2–5pm) in Stephen Street is known for its 'Yeats Room'. It is filled with manuscripts, photographs, letters and other memorabilia relating to his life and work.

The ruins of **Sligo Abbey**, founded in 1252, are also worth a visit, in particular the well preserved stone high altar.

7: The North

Enniskillen – Donegal – Letterkenny – Derry – Omagh – Portrush – Giant's Causeway – Armagh – Newcastle – Newry (approx 950km/600 miles)

Map on pages 82–83

The province of Ulster is composed of nine counties. Six of them (Antrim, Armagh, Derry, Down, Fermanagh and Tyrone) belong to the section of the United Kingdom known as 'Northern Ireland', and the remaining three (Cavan, Donegal and Monaghan) to the Republic. Calling Ulster the north of Ireland is acceptable, geographically speaking, but referring to the political unit of Northern Ireland as 'Ulster' is contentious. In this part of the country, the correct terminology is all-important, and it is often difficult to catch all the nuances (there is no real consensus, for example, on whether Northern Ireland's second-largest town should be called 'Derry' or 'Londonderry'). Locals who refer to their home as 'Ulster' or 'the province' are most probably Protestant unionists. Republicans often use the term 'six counties', implicitly allocating the six to a united Ireland. 'Northern Ireland' is the officially accepted name in polite conversation.

The tourist authorities on either side of the border are doing their best to attract visitors to the dramatic landscapes of the north coast. They have realised that a long insistence on the beauties of

Below: Ballintoy, on Antrim's northern coast
Bottom: Derry people are famed for their friendliness

Below: a master weaver
demonstrates his craft at
Lisburn Museum, Co. Antrim
Bottom: Helen's Bay beach,
north of Belfast

the region and how safe it is for travellers is not as effective as one television report on the 'peace'. Even for people who have holidayed in Ireland for years, there's a new world to discover today.

This route takes in the sandy beaches and mountain passes of Donegal, Italianate palazzos near Enniskillen and the loughs and peninsulas of the north coast. The Giant's Causeway is an extraordinary geological sight steeped in legend, and the Antrim Coast road gives access to what Thackeray called 'Switzerland in miniature'. Towns such as Derry, Strabane, Armagh and Omagh all merit a stop along the way.

ROUTE 7

0   20 km
0   20 miles

Malin Head
Ballyhillin
Ballyliffin
Fanad Head
Glasmullan
Tory Island
Horn Head
Fanad
Dunfanaghy
Buncrana
Bloody Foreland Head
Brinlack
Carrigart
Rathmullan
Falcarragh
Gola Is.
Creeslough
Bunbeg
Speenoge
Aran or
Aranmore Island
The
Rosses
Glenveagh
N.P.
Rathmelton
Grianan of
Aileach
Burtonport
Dunglow
Letterkenny
(Leitir Ceanainn)
A5
Gweebarra Bay
Narin
Fintown
Finn
Kilross
Strabane
Dawros Head
Glenties
Ballybofey
Castlefinn
Ardara
Blue Stack Mtns
Glencolumbkille
Glengesh
Pass
N15
Newtown
stewar
Malin Beg
Killybegs
Inver
Donegal
Killen
Slieve
League
Kilcar
Dunkineely
Pettigoe
Kesh
Dromore
Ballyshannon
Donegal Bay
Bundoran
Belleek
Lower
Lough Erne
A32
Mullaghmore
Killadeas
Inishmurray
Grange
N15
Lough
Melvin
Garrison
Enniskillen
Castle
Coole
Yeats
Grave
Manorhamilton
Belcoo
Drumard
Drumcliff
Sligo
(Sligeach)
N16
Florence
Court
Upper
Lough
Erne
Sligo Bay
Dromahair
Dowra
Templeboy
Ballysadare
Drumkeeran
Lough
Allen
Iron Mtns
Derrynacreeve
Slieve Gamph
or the Ox Mtns
Ropefield
N4
Geevagh
Ballinamore
N17
Tobercurry
Mullany's
Cross
Gorteen
Boyle
Leitrim
Killashandra
IRELAND
(ÉIRE)

INTO DONEGAL

The quickest route from Sligo to Donegal Town leads along the sea coast via the resort of **Bundoran**, which is particularly popular with Northern Irish Catholics. It has amusement arcades, chip shops, and what is allegedly the cleanest beach in Europe, Tullan Strand. Further north, pass through the busy market town of **Ballyshannon** up on its hill above the River Erne. From there, turn left off the N15 on to the R231 to reach the long sandy beach of **Rossnowlagh**. This place isn't often deserted, but only because campers and surfers know how good it is. If the

Farming is still big business

Map
on pages
82–83

Devenish Island

There are very good excursions by boat on Lower Lough Erne, either setting out from Brook Park on the A46 north of Enniskillen town centre, or by the ferry that leaves from Tory Jetty on the A32. Both travel to Devenish Island. Here, there are ruined churches and monasteries (predominantly 12th- to 15th-century), a museum (open Apr–Sept Tues–Sat 10am–6pm, Sun 2–6pm), and an 25-m (80-ft) high round tower which can be climbed for a truly breathtaking panoramic view.

weather cooperates, Donegal Bay can be just the place for a beach holiday.

ENNISKILLEN

A good reason for crossing the Northern Ireland border east of Ballyshannon is the village of **Belleek**, renowned for its dainty pottery. Then continue towards ★ **Enniskillen**, the regional centre of Fermanagh. It is located on Cethlin's Island, once a strategic crossing-point of Lough Erne. The main reason Enniskillen is known internationally is because an IRA bomb exploded here on 11 November 1987 during a remembrance ceremony for the dead of both world wars, and 13 people were killed. For tourists, this town lies at the centre of one of the most attractive holiday regions inland from the coast. Cabin cruisers can be hired here, and sailed the length of Upper Lough Erne (south of the town) or across the expanses of Lower Lough Erne (to the north). Boats can also travel much further now that the Shannon-Erne Waterway is open.

ITALIAN STYLE

A trip down the A4 southeast of Enniskillen and a visit to ★★ **Castle Coole** (open noon–6pm, Mar–May and Sept Sat–Sun, June Wed–Mon July–Aug daily; grounds open daily 10am–4pm, until 8pm May–Sept, free) will transport you back to the elegant Anglo-Irish upper-class life of the late 18th century. This country palazzo, designed in 1790 by James Wyatt, is considered the most successful neoclassical structure in Ireland. The treeless lawn in front of the house does much to reinforce this impression. The harmonious proportions of the inner rooms and the Regency furniture radiate effortless superiority. The main facade is clad in Portland stone, imported from England. ★ **Florence Court** (open Apr, May and Sept Sat–Sun noon–6pm, June–Aug daily 1–6pm), a Palladian country seat, 13km (8 miles) southwest of Enniskillen (signposted from the A32) was built in the mid-

Castle Coole

18th century and contains some marvellous rococo stucco work.

Star Attraction
● Castle Coole

BOA ISLAND

The main road (A46) runs along the southern and western shore of Lower Lough Erne, entering the Republic again near Belleek. A more pleasant route for those with time on their hands leads northeast around the lough (A32/B82).

If you take the latter route, be sure to turn off beyond Kesh on to the A47, which leads via ★ **Boa Island** and thus virtually through the middle of Lough Erne. At the western end of the island a sign on the left points the way to Caldragh Cemetery. Here, you'll find two Celtic statues, the larger of which is often compared with the Roman god Janus because of the two large-eyed faces on either side of the heart-shaped head. It is surprising that these pagan relics have been allowed to remain in a Christian cemetery – and that they stand in the open despite their historical value.

Below: a Janus-headed figure on Boa Island
Bottom: old cottage, Donegal

DONEGAL TOWN

Back on the mainland, **Donegal** can be reached either via Belleek and Ballyshannon or via two smaller roads, the B136 (in Northern Ireland) and the R232 (in the Republic). At the centre

Map
on pages
82–83

of this attractive town is a triangular market square, known as The Diamond, with shops including a good bookstore and Magee's, a chaotic clothes store selling made-to-measure jackets, trousers and caps in Donegal tweed. On a bend in the River Eske in the town centre are the ruins of Donegal Castle, which until the 'Flight of the Earls' in 1607 was the seat of the Princes of Tyrconnell.

SLIEVE LEAGUE

Below: fishing boats, Killybegs
Bottom: the coast between
Burtonport and Ardara

On the northern shore of Donegal Bay we come to another of those stretches of coastline to which no superlative can do justice. The N56 leads westwards out of Donegal Town through the villages of Mountcharles and Dunkineely (the lighthouse at St John's Point on the small promontory stands right in the middle of the bay); turn left on to the R263 towards the fishing harbour of **Killybegs** and continue along the coast. Another good place for a view is Drumcanoo Head, and the bay of Fintragh is also worth exploring.

Things become really spectacular on reaching the 'colourful' rocky cliffs that make up the southern slope of the 600-m (1,970-ft) high mountain of ★★ **Slieve League**. For the best view, follow the signs to Teelin, and from there to Bunglas (the signs to 'Slieve League' lead to the mountain, not

to the view). Down at Teelin Pier, a boat leaves twice a day in the summer, providing a completely different perspective of this stretch of coast.

Star Attraction
● Slieve League

GLENCOLUMBCILLE

★ **Glencolumbcille**, meaning 'valley of Columba', is the name of the valley and the village at its end, even though it appears on some maps as 'Cashel'. St Columba, who later went to Scotland as a missionary and founded the monastery on Iona, was born in Donegal in 521, and this valley is said to have been one of his favourite sights. A ruined chapel and the remains of other buildings, along with a few stone crosses, mark the destination of many pilgrims who come here barefoot on the night of 9 June each year.

The ★ **Folk Village Museum** (open Apr–Sept Mon–Sat 10am–6pm, Sun noon–6pm) in Glencolumbcille comprises three cottages illustrating how the local population lived during the 18th, 19th and early 20th centuries. This is one of the most important *Gaeltacht* regions of the country, and summer courses are held here in the Gaelic language, folk dancing and traditional music.

> **Folk Village Museum**
> The Folk Village Museum at Glencolumbcille, opened in 1967, is one of the oldest of its kind in Ireland. It owes its existence to the priest James McDyer (died 1987), who took over the presbytery in the 1950s. He was so appalled at the 75 percent rate of emigration that he organised several very successful co-operatives (e.g. knitting machines) and encouraged tourism.

Glencolmcille Folk Village Museum

GLENGESH PASS

The road from Glencolumbcille leads over the steep ★ **Glengesh Pass**, offering magnificent views of **Ardara**. This pleasant town is a manufacturing centre for tweed and knitted goods. There were eight shops along its two high streets at last count and there are several other production centres outside the village, which allow visitors inside the workshops and also sell direct to the public. The products are less expensive than in Dublin or London. It's also reassuring to know that the money goes straight to the manufacturer.

DONEGAL'S WEST COAST

The west coast of Donegal is so popular with visitors from Northern Ireland that it is usually crowded in the summer months. The attractive

Map
on pages
82–83

Below: trawlers in Burtonport
Bottom: Glenveagh Castle
gardens

beach of Narin (marked as Naran on some maps) on Dawros Head north of Ardara is a favourite destination because at low tide it's possible to walk across to the tiny island of **Inishkeel**, with its ruined Early Christian monastery.

The coast becomes increasingly jagged from here, with countless tiny islands just offshore, and it's no coincidence that the region to the north of **Dungloe** is known as 'The Rosses' (*Na Rosa* means 'promontory' in Irish).

From the fishing harbour of **Burtonport** a ferry connects with Ireland's 'other' **Aran Island**, also known as Arranmore, which is surprisingly densely populated and relatively prosperous as a result of tourism, fishing and European Union regional subsidies. As with most of the islands along the coast that have natural harbours, Aran bears the signs of centuries-old settlement – this time in the shape of an ancient stone fort on its southern shore.

GLENVEAGH NATIONAL PASS

Travelling round the northwestern corner of Donegal along the well-surfaced coast roads is a rewarding experience, especially when combined with the odd detour to beaches and small harbours along the way – such as near Bunbeg – to Bloody Foreland (so named because of its red

granite cliffs), Falcarragh, Horn Head (with dramatic 180-m/600-ft high cliffs) and the smart little holiday town of **Dunfanaghy**.

It's worth taking a detour inland at this point by following the N56/R251 near Gweedore across the moorland of the Glenveagh National Park to ★ **Glenveagh Castle** (castle and visitors' centre open Apr–Oct daily 10am–6.30pm). This luxurious 'sporting lodge' has quite a history. It was commissioned in 1871 by John George Adair. Queen Victoria's son, Prince Edward, had a stag brought here from Windsor Great Park to increase the stock of game. In 1929 the estate was purchased by the prominent archaeologist, Professor Arthur Kingsley Porter, who set off one day for a walking tour of the island of Inishboffin off the coast of Galway and was never seen again. The next owner was the wealthy American, Henry McIlhenny, whose family came from Donegal. He landscaped the magnificent gardens around the house and made the property over to the Irish state in 1983.

AROUND LOUGH SWILLY

The two peninsulas of Fanad and Inishowen, together making up the northeast of Donegal, are separated by **Lough Swilly** which cuts deep inland. The road on the western shore of the lough grows increasingly narrow and remote until it reaches Fanad Head. On the way, **Rathmullan**, is a charming resort with a popular beach and also a good hotel, Rathmullan House *(see page 126)*.

North of the town the road climbs high above the coast before suddenly descending towards the sea in a series of steep hairpin bends. Keep your eyes on the road even though it is hard to ignore the fantastic views of one of the best beaches in the area down in ★ **Ballymastocker Bay**.

GRIANÁN OF AILEACH

The busy administrative centre of Donegal is **Letterkenny**, at the southernmost point of Lough Swilly. The Tourist Information Office here in

Letterkenny music fest
Letterkenny hosts a four-day-long music festival in August, featuring jazz, rock, folk and also a busking (street music) contest. The pubs on the main street – reputedly the longest in Ireland – provide abundant entertainment at other times of year, too.

Glenveagh Castle

Map
on pages
82–83

Below: the Grianán of Aileach
Bottom: Inishowen Peninsula,
Malin Head

Derry Road is responsible for information and advance booking of accommodation for the entire northwestern region.

To get from Letterkenny to the eastern shore of Lough Swilly and the northernmost point of the Irish mainland, ★ **Malin Head**, travel along the N13 in the direction of Derry and – just before the border crossing – turn off along the R238 in the direction of Buncrana.

Before this turning, look out for an unnumbered minor road on the right signposted to the ★★ **Grianán of Aileach**. The round fort, on its 230-m (750-ft) high mound, provides a spectacular panoramic view of the surrounding countryside that extends as far as Derry when the weather is good.

The fortress wall is surrounded by traces of prehistoric earthworks, but the stone structure itself probably dates from the Christian era. The princes of the Gaelic O'Neill clan used this fort as their residence from the 5th century onwards until it was razed to the ground in 1101 by Murtaugh O'Brien, the king of Munster. It looks so well-preserved today only because of an extensive facelift carried out around 1870, which has been strongly criticised by many modern archaeologists. The widespread theory that the complex may have served as a solar temple should be taken with a pinch of salt.

DERRY

On the other side of the Northern Irish border, at the mouth of the River Foyle, lies ★ **Derry** (pop. 100,000), the second-largest city in Northern Ireland. The name 'Londonderry' is only used by Protestants these days to help keep alive the link with Britain; in everyday life almost all the locals refer to the place as Derry, plain and simple.

The history of the name is interesting. Derry was originally the Irish *Doire* (oak grove); this became 'Londonderry' in 1613 when James I granted large areas of the town to London guilds, who duly financed the fortifications and planned the town the way it looks today.

The pro-British Unionists are still very proud of the Protestant guildsmen who helped the town to withstand a siege by James II's troops for 105 days in 1689, thus allowing William of Orange time to assemble his army. Centuries of Protestant supremacy forced the Ulster Catholic population to move out into the suburbs, and denied them any administrative responsibility.

DERRY CITY CENTRE

As in the case of Belfast, Derry's residential suburbs are divided by religion: northwest of the old city is the Catholic region of Bogside, and on the other side of the river is the Protestant area, Waterside. The old city centre on a hill above the River Foyle is surrounded by a wall, dating from the early 17th century, which gave rise to Derry's local nickname of 'the Maiden City' – because, despite several sieges, it was never successfully taken.

At the centre of the city lies a generously proportioned main square, The Diamond, from which Shipquay Street descends steeply to Shipquay Gate by the river. On the right-hand side is a modern shopping centre, and on the left are passages leading to narrow winding streets with small shops and cafés. The ★ **Tower Museum** (open Sept–June Tues–Sat 10am–5pm; July–Aug Mon–Sat 10am–5pm, Sun 2–5pm) in the O'Doherty Tower Interpretive Centre next to Shipquay Gate

Star Attraction
● Grianán of Aileach

The trickiest of names
During the bitter fighting of the 1960s, '70s and '80s, which reached its climax with the deaths of 13 Catholic civil rights demonstators at the hands of British paratroops in 1972, the name of Londonderry was on every politician's lips. In the local elections in 1985 the nationalist SDLP and Sinn Féin achieved a majority in the municipal council and the city's name was officially changed to Derry. Travel brochures still bear both names in an attempt not to overly offend the resident Protestant population. On the other hand, the county in which the town is situated is still generally referred to as Londonderry.

A cannon atop Derry's walls

Map
on pages
82–83

Letters from Strabane
Two printers from Strabane influenced American history: one was James Wilson, grandfather of President Woodrow Wilson, who emigrated in 1807; the other was John Dunlap, who emigrated in 1771 and founded a printing works in America that published the American Declaration of Independence in 1776. Dunlap brought out the first American daily newspaper in 1784. Another of the town's sons is Flann O'Brien (1911–66), who earned his living in Dublin from the printed word; he has been referred to by some as 'the drinking man's Joyce'.

Glenelly Valley in the Sperrins

has won several prizes for its exhibition technology, and also for its presentation of different versions of the city's history (rather than any attempt to create a 'balanced' one).

STRABANE

Before exploring the north coast, it's worth taking a detour inland. Drive south from Derry along the River Foyle into County Tyrone. The busy little town of **Strabane** has been known for its textile industry for more than two centuries, and even though the linen industry has now declined massively in importance, the town still manufactures shirts and tights.

During the 18th and 19th centuries Strabane was also a centre of the printing industry. At one time there were two newspapers here and 10 printing works. ★ **Gray's Printing Press** (open Tues–Fri 11am–5pm, Sat 11.30am–5pm), in an elegant Georgian building on Main Street, features a 19th-century print shop, a stationer and a fascinating audio-visual presentation on the history of the local printing industry.

SPERRIN MOUNTAINS

A region to explore to the east of Strabane contains the beautiful green wooded hills known as the **Sperrin Mountains**, on the northern bank of the River Glenelly. On a hike here you may come across the odd prospector panning for gold – even the early Celts knew gold was here.

The tourist information centre in Strabane provides hiking maps, and the **Sperrin Heritage Centre** (open Apr–Oct Mon–Fri 11.30am–5.30pm, Sat 11.30am–6pm, Sun 2–6pm), on the B47 between Cranagh and Sperrin, contains several exhibits on the flora and fauna of the region.

ULSTER-AMERICAN FOLK PARK

The route eastwards through the Sperrins leads to the northern end of Lough Neagh, where you can turn back north again. However, it's worth driving south from Strabane on the A5, because just north of Omagh is the ★ **Ulster-American Folk Park** (open Easter–Sept Mon–Sat 11am–6.30pm, Sun 11am–6.30pm; Oct–Easter Mon–Fri 10.30am–5pm). This open-air museum documents Ulster's contribution to American history – no less than five signatories to the Declaration of Independence came from the province. The exhibits include reconstructions of Irish and American houses from the 18th and 19th centuries and a life-sized cutaway model of an emigrant ship. People in costume display various crafts.

LOUGH NEAGH

The town of **Omagh** is a pleasant placeon the River Strule. But the peace here was shattered on 15 August 1998, when a Republican splinter group detonated a car bomb in the town centre, which was crowded with Saturday shoppers. Twenty-nine people died and hundreds were injured in this, the single worst atrocity perpetrated in Northern Ireland since the late 1960s.

From Omagh, take the well-surfaced A505 to Cookstown and continue on to the western shore of **Lough Neagh**. The lough (400sq km/154sq miles) is the largest lake in the British Isles. It is known for its eels, which are caught throughout the summer, from May onwards, by

Below: blacksmith at the Ulster-American Folk Park
Bottom: the colourful houses of Derry

Map
on pages
82–83

professional fishermen using lines and nets. At peak season thousands of eels a day get hauled up on to the sandy shore of the lough.

To the east of Cookstown, on the shore of Lough Neagh (turn right at the end of the B73), are the ruins of the 6th-century monastery complex of **Ardboe**, with one of the finest and best-preserved high crosses in Ireland. The ★ **Ardboe Cross**, hewn from sandstone during the 10th century, stands more than 5m (16ft) high. It is decorated with 22 biblical scenes – the west side shows the New Testament, the east side is the Old.

On the western side of the lough, in the valley of the River Bann, the A54 leads via **Coleraine**, a traffic junction with good shops, to the north coast from Derry and Antrim, but a short detour will take you to **Limavady**.

DOWNHILL

A gem of aristocratic eccentricity can be admired on the steep coast just north of Limavady. ★★ **Downhill** (open all year) is a large park set amid spectacular scenery, with ruins, monuments and temples. It was laid out between 1774 and 1788 on the orders of Frederick Hervey, the count of Bristol, who later became the bishop of Derry.

Hervey appears to have been a very untypical clergyman: his personal wealth allowed him to travel first-class all over Europe, and anyone wondering why there are so many luxury establishments called 'Hotel Bristol' in Venice, Zermatt, Vienna and Paris will find the answer in Frederick Hervey's travel fever. Back home, he organised horse races beneath the cliffs for his priests.

Downhill consists of two very ornamental gates, Lion Gate and the Bishop's Gate, which leads into the park; a walled garden; a monument to the count's eldest brother, known as the Mausoleum; the massive ruins of the house itself (the neoclassical Downhill House was destroyed in a fire in 1851); and the spectacular little ★ **Mussenden Temple** (open July–Aug noon–6pm) perched on a rocky crag above the coast. The latter, which was modelled after the Temple of

The 10th-century Ardboe Cross

Vesta in Tivoli, was used by the count as a 'summer library' and is named after his cousin. In Downhill Forest there are lovely walks, a fishpond and waterfalls.

THE CAUSEWAY COAST

The nearby resorts of **Portstewart** and **Portrush** lie on either side of the border between County Londonderry and County Antrim. In the summer they are usually crowded with tourists and trippers from Belfast, but they are a good base for exploring the region because, apart from the usual amusement arcades and fish-and-chip shops, there are pleasant hotels, stores and several attractive sandy beaches.

For a small fee it's possible to drive your car along the 5-km (3-mile) long Portstewart Strand. Even though around 1,000 cars may already have been counted on a hot summer day, the beach never seems especially overcrowded; not that the motor traffic does anything to improve its appearance.

For many years it was extremely rare to meet anyone from the Continent along this coast. Naturally, the Giant's Causeway attracted not only Americans but also French, Dutch and Germans, but they usually came across the border for one or two days at the most, from Donegal, Sligo or Galway. The hotels and bed-and-breakfasts

Below: the Mussenden Temple, Downhill
Bottom: Portstewart harbour

Map
on pages
82–83

Ballycastle Fair

At the eastern end of the Causeway Coast is Ballycastle, Portrush's opposite number. On the last Monday and Tuesday in August, this popular resort town celebrates one of the oldest fairs in Ireland – a fair has been held here every year since 1606. The locals associate it with two special foods: a soft cream sweet known as 'Yellowman' and dried and salted seaweed called 'dulse'.

Bushmills Distillery

around here have been doing far better business since the mid-1990s, when tourism in Northern Ireland began to bring in an extra 20 percent of earnings. But there has been much criticism of what's on offer; the press has even accused the region of being 30 years behind the requirements of modern tourism.

The seaside resorts have much in common with those on the coast of England: the buildings are mainly Victorian (late 19th-century), there are innumerable guesthouses, but there are fewer pubs than in the holiday regions along the south-west coast of Ireland.

There is no shortage of picturesque sights: ★**Dunluce Castle** (open Apr, May and Sept Mon–Sat 10am–6pm, Sun 2–6pm; June–Aug Mon–Sat 10am–6pm, Sun 11am–6pm; Oct–Mar Tues–Sat 10am–4pm, Sun 2–4pm), for instance, is an impressive ruin perched on a rocky headland high above the sea. Most of the complex dates from the 16th century, although castles have stood on this site since at least 1300. It was abandoned in 1641.

The graveyard of the nearby ruined church was the burial ground for sailors from the Spanish Armada galleass *Girona*, which sank off the coast in 1588 with 1,300 men aboard. Treasures from the wreck can be seen in the Ulster Museum in Belfast *(see page 105)*.

WHISKEY GALORE

In **Bushmills**, the whiskey distillery of the same name is open to the public (Apr–Oct Mon–Sat 9.30am–5.30pm, Sun noon–5.30pm; Nov–Mar Mon–Fri 10.30am–3.30pm).

The drink has been produced here since 1608, when James I granted the establishment a licence for the distillation of '*aquavite, usquabagh* and *aqua composite*'. The most famous whiskey from Bushmills, Black Bush, is much revered throughout Ireland. It is made from local barley and the water of St Columb's Rill. The main difference between Scotch whisky and Irish whiskey, apart from the spelling, is that Scotch whisky is distilled twice and Irish three times.

GIANT'S CAUSEWAY

The amazing rock formation known as the ★★★ **Giant's Causeway** is composed of around 37,000 mainly hexagonal basalt columns. Legend has it that the giant Finn MacCumhail (also known as Finn MacCool) built a roadway to Scotland here, and there are indeed very similar rock formations on the Scottish island of Staffa. The scientists, however, say that the Giant's Causeway was created by the rapid cooling of lava flows on their way to the sea around 60 million years ago.

The geological explanation can be analysed at the Visitors' Centre (open May–Oct daily 10am–5pm; June until 5.30pm; July–Aug until 7pm), where there is a café and souvenir shops. The rocks themselves are around a mile away from the nearest car park and can be reached only on foot or by official bus, which is equipped with an electric lift for wheelchairs.

ANTRIM COAST

It's a good idea to head southwest in the direction of Belfast along the ★★ **Antrim Coast Road** (A2), which winds past some magnificent steep scenery. The brown moorlands and rocks of white limestone, black basalt and red sandstone contrast dramatically with the blue sea. The coastal road is a feat of 19th-century engineering. It was designed in 1834 by

Star Attractions
● Giant's Causeway
● Antrim Coast Road

Below: the Giant's Causeway
Bottom: view from the
Antrim Coast Road

Map
on pages
82–83

Sea life
Strangford Lough is a nature reserve, and home to many varieties of seabirds as well as the largest seal colony in Ireland.

Below: Carrickfergus Castle
Bottom: Armagh is known for its Georgian architecture

Sir Charles Lanyon as a work of famine relief and provides access to Antrim's nine glens. Glengariff Glen was likened by the novelist William Makepeace Thackeray to a miniature Switzerland.

Just beyond Ballycastle, if you take the minor road signposted to **Cushendun**, and stay on it until you rejoin the A2 near **Cushendall**, the 'capital of the glens', you'll pass through a particularly fine stretch of landscape. Cushendall is a pleasant village for a short break. A satisfying place for a spot of reflection is the 300-year-old pub called P. J. McCollam in Mill Street.

Further along the route is **Larne**, the ferry harbour for the crossing to Scotland, which marks the end of the magnificent coastal route and a return to the world of dreary suburbs. Between Larne and Belfast, the coastal port of **Carrickfergus** has Ireland's best preserved Norman castle.

ARMAGH

As an optional detour to the southwest of Belfast, take the M1 motorway towards the Fermanagh lakelands, passing farmland and small market towns. One such town, **Armagh**, 61km (38 miles) from Belfast, is graced with Georgian architecture, two cathedrals (one Protestant, one Catholic, naturally), an Ionic-pillared county museum, an enterprising planetarium and the Palace Stables Heritage Centre which recreates the building's life in 1776, complete with carriage rides.

To the west of the city is **Navan Fort**, capital of the kings of Ulster from 300BC. Until recently it was a neglected antiquity; now it has hands-on computers and audio-visual displays.

THE ARDS PENINSULA

Southeast of Belfast, in County Down, lies the relaxing ★**Ards Peninsula**, which separates Strangford Lough from the open sea. The famous landscape garden of **Mount Stewart** (open Apr–Sept daily 1–6pm; Oct–Mar weekends only) is linked to an 18th-century manor house, the childhood home of Lord Castlereagh, a British foreign secretary in the early 19th century.

At the southernmost point of the Ards Peninsula is the pleasant town of ★ **Portaferry**, which has a good hotel. From here take the car ferry to Strangford, after which there's a choice of either following the coast or going via Downpatrick, past the ruins of **Dundrum Castle**, to the locally popular and pretty resort of ★ **Newcastle**.

THE MOUNTAINS OF MOURNE

Beyond Newcastle rise the majestic peaks of the ★★ **Mountains of Mourne**, an astonishingly wild and unspoilt region with numerous challenging hiking routes. The Mourne Countryside Centre on the Central Promenade in Newcastle can provide detailed maps, and it also contains exhibitions documenting local history and ecology.

Only one road crosses the mountains. Take the B180 from Newcastle to Hilltown, and around 7km (4 miles) along it turn left on the B27 towards **Kilkeel**. Those taking this route will have to drive back north again once they arrive at Carlingford Lough to reach the market town of **Newry** and the main road to Dundalk and Dublin. An option is to go back along less-travelled minor roads near Omeath in the Republic and then take the route around the pretty Cooley Peninsula, which eventually reaches Dundalk in a more roundabout way.

Star Attraction
● **Mountains of Mourne**

Below: Strangford Lough has a large seal colony
Bottom: Mount Stewart

Map
on page
102

8: Belfast

When in May 1997 Dame Kiri Te Kanawa inaugurated Belfast's Waterfront Hall by performing Puccini to £80-a-ticket guests, the city's 30 years of troubles seemed a long way away. The 'peace process' had encouraged Belfast to polish up its image: buildings were restored and 'reunification' initiatives discussed.

Tensions between the nationalist and loyalist communities continue, particularly in the western suburbs around the Falls Road and the Shankill Road, separated by the so-called 'Peace Line' wall. But even the traditional trouble spots have become tourist attractions. CityBus's *Belfast: A Living History* tour, for example, takes you past those colourful gable-end murals promoting the causes of the various paramilitary factions. The peace process has had its ups and downs, but the atmosphere is relaxed most of the time. Visitors to the city centre will find the familiar range of British chain stores, and often only the fact that patrolling policemen are conspicuously armed will remind them that this has been the scene of so many terrorist outrages.

Living history

Experience a vanishing way of life at the Ulster Folk and Transport Museum at Holywood, on the northeast outskirts of Belfast. Exhibits include a typical Ulster town from around 1910, complete with reconstructed cottages and farmhouses, a bank, a school, churches and a printer's workshop. The focus on transport includes an exhibition on Belfast's most famous disaster: the Titanic. (Open Mar–June Mon–Fri 10am–5pm, Sat until 6pm, Sun 11am–6pm; July–Sept Mon–Sat 10am–6pm, Sun 11am–6pm; Oct–Feb Mon–Fri 10am–4pm, Sat until 5pm, Sun 11am–5pm.)

Belfast peace mural

HISTORY

Historically, Belfast is Ireland's only industrial city, and seems at first sight to have more in common with Glasgow or Manchester than Dublin. Something that is scarcely ever seen on television reports, however, is Belfast's picturesque location. The hills to the north and west afford good views of the city, and to the east of the centre of Belfast there are attractive lines of buildings along the River Lagan, which flows into Belfast Lough.

The name Belfast is derived from the Irish *Béal feirste*, 'estuary on the sandbank'. The area was first settled in 1177, when the Anglo-Norman John de Courcy built a fort beside the river and a village grew up around it. From the beginning of the 17th century, as part of the 'Ulster Plantation' *(see Historical Highlights, page 16),* Protestant settlers arrived here from southwest

England and Scotland. They were followed by Huguenots, whose linen manufacture laid the foundations of the city's textile industry.

The natural harbour made maritime trade a simple matter; textiles were exported, tobacco imported. The 19th century saw the development of mechanical engineering and shipbuilding; for many years Harland & Wolff was one of the most advanced and successful shipyards in the world. It was here that the 'unsinkable' *Titanic* was built in 1912.

At the beginning of the 20th century Belfast had just as many inhabitants as Dublin, and from an economic point of view it was considerably more important. Belfast has been the capital of Northern Ireland since 1922. Protestant domination of the political and economic sphere caused increasing unrest among Catholics, and from 1969 onwards reports and pictures of the 'troubles' in Belfast went round the world.

CITY TOUR

At the centre of Belfast, ★ **Donegall Square**, with the imposing architecture of **City Hall ❶** and the statues of Queen Victoria, is remarkably reminiscent of George Square in Glasgow or Albert Square in Manchester. All three were built within the space of 20 years (Belfast's City Hall came last – it was begun in 1896) and testify to the immense self-con-

Below: stained-glass window in Belfast City Hall
Bottom: Linenhall Library

Map below

fidence of Victorian Britain. It had the largest colonial empire in the world (there is an exact replica of Belfast's City Hall building in Durban, South Africa) and was the most important of the industrialised nations. This is also reflected in the majestic interior of City Hall, which can be viewed on guided tours (June–Sept Mon–Fri 11am, 2 and 3pm, Sat 2.30pm; Oct– May Mon–Fri 11am and 2.30pm, Sat 2.30pm; tel: 028 9032 0202).

City Hall is flanked by the extravagant Scottish Provident Building and the Pearl Assurance Building.

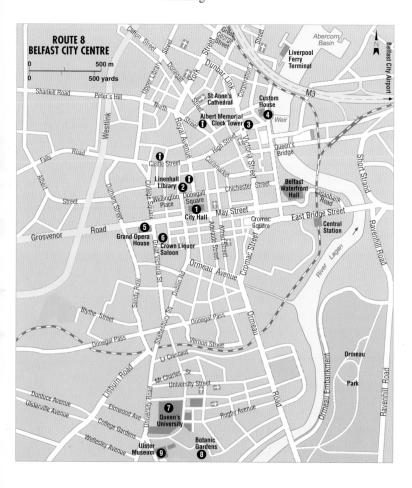

ROUTE 8
BELFAST CITY CENTRE

0   500 m
0   500 yards

LINENHALL LIBRARY

No visitor to Belfast with an interest in the city's more recent history should miss a look inside the ★**Linenhall Library** ❷ (open Mon–Fri 9.30am–5.30pm, Sat 9.30am–4pm) at the north-western corner of Donegall Square. Built in 1864, the library contains a collection of almost every piece of documentation in existence regarding the troubles of the past 30 years – from newspaper articles to posters and postcards. There is a very pleasant wood-panelled reading room in the building and a café on the first floor.

Thomas Russell, first librarian of Linenhall Library, played a leading role in the United Irishmen's struggle for democratic reforms. Caught after a rebellion in 1803, he was hanged ouside Downpatrick's jail. Mary McCracken, a fellow member of the movement who had long been in love with Russell, watched from below, vainly hoping he would not perish. After the crowd dispersed, Mary took his body to St Margaret's churchyard where he is now buried. Legend has it that Mary's ghost visits every 21 October to lay a single flower on his grave.

To the north of Donegall Square an entire city quarter around the Cornmarket, with two modern shopping centres, has been turned into a pedestrian precinct. **The Entries** is the name given to the alleyways connecting the streets. This area used to be home to several craftsmen and artisans. These days the Entries are best known for their pubs, including the oldest one in the city, White's Tavern in Winecellar Entry (1630).

At the northeastern end of the High Street is the **Albert Memorial Clock Tower** ❸, which is closed to visitors because the foundations are visibly subsiding. Continue east to the **Custom House** ❹, with its dignified facade, on the bank of the River Lagan. After retracing your steps to the Albert Clock, head to the northwest along Victoria Street then Waring and finally Donegall Street to ★**St Anne's Cathedral** (open Mon–Sat 10am–4pm; Sun before and after services). It was opened in 1890 and completed nearly a century later. The baptistry is by a local architect, W. H.

Historical Joy's Entry
Francis Joy founded the Belfast Newsletter in 1737 under the 'sign of the Peacock' on Bridge Street. The Peacock symbol is still synonymous with the paper now the oldest newspaper still in circulation in the Brish Isles. This paper, begun in humble Joy's Entry has the rare distinction of constant publication in four different centuries.

Linenhall Street, looking towards the City Hall

Map on page 102

Map on page 102

St George's Market
Open on Friday morning and on the first and third Saturday in the month for a farmer's market, this trading place on May Street is more than 100 years old. Recently restored, it sells everything, from fresh fish and produce to second-hand videos.

Lynn; Gertrude Stein created the mosaics. Walking west from the cathedral, you will arrive at the Castle Court shopping centre. This enormous modern building contains Smithfield Market, where all kinds of junk and old books are on sale.

From King Street, cross College Square and go south along Great Victoria Street, passing several classical Victorian buildings. The **Old Museum** (Ireland's oldest, built in 1830) today contains a cultural centre and a theatre. The **Grand Opera House ❺** stages operas, musicals and plays in an Oriental-style building designed by Frank Matcham in 1897.

OUT OF THE CENTRE

The most frequently photographed pub in Belfast is the ★ **Crown Liquor Saloon ❻** in Great Victoria Street. Its richly ornamented tile-and-glass facade and tiled interior have earned it listed building status, but customers are still served here just as they would be in any other pub.

Walking south, beyond Shaftesbury Square it's worth making a brief detour to take a look at the neoclassical townhouses in Lower Crescent, Crescent Gardens and Upper Crescent, which date from the early 19th century. The nearer one gets to the university area, the more elegant the buildings become – the villas in the parallel Mount Charles Street and University Street also merit closer inspection.

The main building at ★ **Queen's University ❼** was designed in Early Victorian style by Charles Lanyon, the architect responsible for the Linenhall Library and the Custom House. Today, almost all the Victorian terraced houses nearby are occupied by university departments.

THE SOUTHERN SIGHTS

South of the university are the magnificent ★ **Botanic Gardens ❽** (open daily until sunset, greenhouses Apr–Aug Mon–Fri 10am–5pm, Sat–Sun 1–5pm; Sept–Mar Mon–Fri 10am–4pm, Sat–Sun 2–4pm), with the graceful silhouette of the Palm House at the centre. It was erected in 1831.

The ornate Grand Opera House

The **★★Ulster Museum ❾** (open Mon–Fri 10am–5pm, Sat 1–5pm, Sun 2–5pm) acts as a Northern Irish national museum of archaeological, cultural and industrial history. The highlights here include finds from the Spanish Armada ship *Girona*, which sank off the Antrim coast in 1588 *(see page 96)*, and exhibits documenting historical events from the Bronze Age to the Industrial Revolution. The fine arts collection on the first floor has several good watercolours, drawings, engravings and sketches by Irish and British artists such as Edward Lear, William Henry Hunt and Thomas Rowlandson.

EXCURSION TO CAVE HILL

A worthwhile excursion outside Belfast is to ★**Cave Hill**, a short bus ride to the north (bus No 45 from Donegall Square). This hill affords far-reaching views of the city and the bay. The well-tended gardens of **Belfast Castle** (open for tours when not being used for functions; tel: 028-90776925) lie on its southeastern slopes. The castle was completed in 1870 in Scottish Baronial style and is modelled after Balmoral.

At the northeastern end of Cave Hill is **Belfast Zoo** (open daily 10am–5pm, winter 10am–2.30pm), which has an admirable captive breeding programme for rare animals.

Star Attraction
● Ulster Museum

Below: ornate decorations in the Crown Liquor Saloon
Bottom: the Lagan towpath near Belfast

Architecture

The archetypal Celtic ornamentation can be admired in innumerable books about Ireland, and ranges from the metalwork on the Tara Brooch to the 8th-century Ardagh Goblet. A high point in the production of European illuminated manuscripts was reached with the celebrated *Book of Kells (see page 24)* in the 9th century.

Romanesque and, later, Gothic churches appeared from the 11th century, including Cormac's Chapel, Cashel, and Black Abbey, Kilkenny. When the Anglo-Normans colonised Ireland during the 12th century they brought their unmistakable defensive architecture with them (Trim Castle, Bunratty Castle), and later immigrants copied the designs. Fortified Scottish-style towered buildings were erected in Ulster during the 17th century.

From the 18th century, Irish architecture was characterised by the neoclassical, such as Palladianism. The ideas were mainly imported, but some Irish architects made important contributions, especially in Dublin: Thomas Burgh (born 1670) designed the library of Trinity College, and Sir Edward Lovett Pearce (born 1699) was responsible for Parliament House. Later, several English architects rose to prominence: James Gandon (born 1743) from London built the Custom House and the Four Courts in Dublin, and James Wyatt (born 1746) from Staffordshire, also known as 'Wyatt the Destroyer' because of his penchant for radical alteration, designed several country estates such as the magnificent Castle Coole *(see page 84)*.

Anglo-Irish rule introduced Victorian monumentalism to Ireland in the mid-19th century: numerous banks, country houses and churches were rebuilt in the neoclassical style, or were altered to reflect the latest trends. Tullira Castle in Galway, a 17th-century tower house, was transformed into a mock-Tudor palace around 1880; St Finbarr's Cathedral in Cork is an extraordinary neo-Gothic construction. Twentieth-century Modernism took some time to reach Ireland (Dublin Airport, built by Desmond FitzGerald in 1941, is an example). Most visitors these days are surprised by the large number of modern churches in the country.

Opposite: Powerscourt House and Gardens, Co. Wicklow

Below: Blarney Castle
Bottom: the quad at Trinity College, Dublin

W.B. Yeats's epitaph, Drumcliffe cemetery

LITERATURE

Ireland has produced literary works in both Gaelic and English. Gaelic literature flourished from the Early Christian period until the suppression of Gaelic in the 17th and 18th centuries. Sagas and legends in Old Irish (*ca* AD600–900) have been preserved in manuscripts written far later. One epic, *Táin Bó Cuailnge (The Cattle Theft at Cooley)*, recounts the adventures of the young hero Cú Chulainn and his adversary Queen Maeve of Connaught. Geoffrey Keating (1570–1645) wrote prose that was stylistically exemplary (*Foras Feasa ar Éirinn/History of Ireland*); and one of the last great Classical Irish poets was Aodhgan Ó Raithille (born 1675), whose works reflect his knowledge that his culture was in decline. The Celtic Revival of the late 19th century brought modern Gaelic literature to a broad reading public. Tales by Blasket islanders such as Tómas ó Crohan (1856–1937) and Peig Sayers (1873–1958) were published in the original and in translation. The most important academically trained author writing in Gaelic in the 20th century was Máirtin O'Cadhain (1906–70).

Literary historians still argue whether authors during the Protestant Ascendancy such as Nathum Tate (1652–1715) or the great Jonathan Swift (1667–1745) should, despite the 'accident' of their Irish birth, really be placed under the heading of English literature. Ireland's disproportionately large contribution to the London theatre scene during the 18th century is telling: William Congreve (1670–1729), George Farquhar (1678–1707), Oliver Goldsmith (1728–74) and Richard Brinsley Sheridan (1751–1816) are just a few of the most outstanding dramatists.

One successful female author at the end of the 18th century was Maria Edgeworth (1767–1849), whose first novel, *Castle Rackrent*, influenced Sir Walter Scott and Turgenev as well as being an impressive and accurate description of the excesses of the Anglo-Irish nobility.

For the literary historians, Oscar Wilde (1854–1900) and George Bernard Shaw (1856–1950) are placed in the same category as Jonathan Swift:

their powerful language and irony is attributed to their Irish origins, but they spent most of their lives in London literary circles and dealt only rarely with Irish topics.

Other examples of Anglo-Irish literature include Lady Isabella Gregory (1852–1932), William Butler Yeats (1865–1939), John Millington Synge (1871–1909) and Sean O'Casey (1884–1964). All strengthened Irish drama.

James Joyce (1882–1941) wrote his epochal novel *Ulysses* between 1914 and 1921 in Trieste, Zurich and Paris. Today it is the most famous in a long line of works written by Irish authors who have penned detailed descriptions of their home country while living abroad – among them William Trevor (born 1928) and Edna O'Brien (born 1930). Modern exponents of Irish literature who have achieved a worldwide reputation include Samuel Beckett (1906–89), who lived mostly in France from 1932 and examined in his plays (notably *Waiting for Godot*) the pointlessness of human life; the dramatist Brian Friel (born 1929, *Philadelphia, Here I Come* and *Dancing at Lughnasa*) and the novelist Roddy Doyle (born 1958), whose book *The Commitments* was filmed by Alan Parker.

The poet Seamus Heaney (born 1939) was the fourth Irishman after Yeats, Shaw and Beckett to receive the Nobel Prize for Literature.

Below: James Joyce surveys Dublin's city centre
Bottom: a costumed Dubliner celebrates Bloomsday from Joyce's novel Ulysses

Festivals

February Dublin Film Festival, usually held at the end of the month and into March. It premieres Irish and international movies.

March St Patrick's Day (17 March): celebrations held throughout Ireland for the feast of the nation's patron saint; street parades in Dublin; traditional music festivals countrywide. The World Irish Dancing Championships in Dublin.

May Pan Celtic Week in Killarney at which Celtic descendants from Brittany, Cornwall, Wales, Scotland and Ireland come together.

June Bloomsday Literary Festival (16 June) is a celebration of the author James Joyce. Staged in Dublin, it features a pilgrimage around the city visiting all the places mentioned in *Ulysses*, as well as readings from the author's landmark novel. The Irish Derby, the biggest event of the horse-racing calendar, is held in The Curragh, County Kildare.

August Dublin Horse Show, the country's most important show-jumping event. The Puck Fair, held in Kilorgin, Kerry, is an ancient pagan festival lasting three days, during which there is much drinking and carousing, and a goat is crowned king of the village. Fleadh Ceoil Na h'Eireann is an all-Ireland festival of culture and music.

September The Match-Making Festival in Lisdoonvarna, County Clare, is much more fun than computer dating. Oyster festivals are held in Galway and Clarinbridge. Dublin Theatre Festival (September–October).

October Wexford Opera Festival. This two-week jamboree is Ireland's top opera event.

JAMES JOYCE'S ULYSSES

There are people who come to Dublin for no other reason than to follow the trail of James Joyce (1882–1941) and his great work *Ulysses*, which tracks Stephen Daedalus and Leopold Bloom on 16 June 1904. This date is celebrated each year as 'Bloomsday' with readings, Edwardian dress and many visits to pubs mentioned in the book.

No 35, North Great George's Street, east of Parnell Square, houses the James Joyce Centre (tel: 873 1984), a small museum which organises guided tours through Joyce's Dublin. The James Joyce Museum (Joyce Tower; Sandycove, near Dun Laoghaire, open Feb–Oct Mon–Sat 10am–1pm and 2–5pm, Sun 2–6pm; bus No. 8 from Eden Quay in the city centre) contains much memorabilia and is attractively situated. A helpful book on the subject is *The Ulysses Guide* (London 1988) by Robert Nicholson; and those eager to delve even more deeply into the subject should read the fascinating *James Joyce's Ireland* (New Haven/London 1992) by David Pierce. The handbook for connoisseurs continues to be Richard Ellman's classic study *Ulysses on the Liffey* (London 1972).

Music

The Irish draw a sharp distinction between traditional music and folk music. Traditional music comprises instrumental airs and dances such as jigs and reels on the one hand and unaccompanied singing on the other. Traditional instruments include the Uilleann pipes, the fiddle and the flute, and the tunes and airs are often played in unison.

Regional peculiarities are proudly emphasised: in Clare the most popular line-up is accordion and tin whistle; Donegal is famous for its fiddlers; and Sligo music is full of ornamentation and rhythmic oddities. Musicians are proud of their ability to improvise and of never playing the same tune twice. The same applies to singing 'in the old style' (*sean-nós*): songs from Connemara often stay within one octave whereas Kerry songs have simpler melodies but a broader tonal range.

All this has very little to do with the 'folk

music' heard in pubs during the summer months and tailored to tourists' expectations. The instruments here can include guitars, bouzoukis, banjos and even synthesizers. Groups such as The Dubliners and Altan have done much to make this music internationally popular. Anyone lucky enough to run across a traditional session in Clare or Donegal, featuring local musicians, will be amazed at how special (and often bizarre) an experience it is.

*Below: making music
Bottom: making a bodhran,
a goatskin tambourine*

ROCK AND POP IN DUBLIN

In certain circles Dublin is known as 'the city of a thousand bands'. For several years it has been regarded as one of Europe's leading rock and pop centres.

Names such as Thin Lizzy or The Boomtown Rats may ring a bell with the older generation, but it was the massive success enjoyed by the group U2 that first brought Dublin to international notice in the music business. U2 has always insisted on living and recording in its home city, and promotes many local bands such as In Tua Nua.

The best guides to what's going on in rock and pop are the city magazine *In Dublin* and the music magazine *Hot Press*. Alternatively, you can visit one of many music sites on the Internet (*Dublin live*, www.ireland.com/dublin).

FOOD AND DRINK

The common view of Irish food is often overshadowed by notions of a bitterly poor country that was colonised for far too long by a rich country devoid of culinary traditions. Although this is partially true, and Ireland isn't exactly the top address for European gourmets, visitors should not worry unduly about finding good food – though it may seem expensive.

All the larger towns contain a good selection of restaurants, many of them up to international standards, and the better hotels out in the country also take the trouble to produce good food with fresh local ingredients. Today there are gastronomic delights waiting in every corner of the island. As with everywhere else it's best to seek advice to avoid disappointment. Alongside the annually updated *Michelin* and *Georgina Campbell's Jameson* guides (the latter contains detailed information on about 600 hotels, restaurants and pubs of all price categories) one publication is invaluable: the *Bridgestone Irish Food Guide*. It not only describes restaurants and pubs but also where to find special foods; the numerous features, covering a host of topics, are also very interesting. The publishers (Estragon Press) also do a *Bridgestone Vegetarian's Guide to Ireland*.

Those keen on self-catering holidays can, of course, buy Irish ingredients and try out a few Irish recipes themselves, but the best Irish food is usually enjoyed by those staying at Bed and Breakfasts or holidaying on farms (*see Accommodation, page 123*). It soon becomes clear that all the press reports are right: the Irish *do* eat too much (163 percent of the recommended intake of calories daily). It begins with breakfast: the egg, bacon and sausage is often joined by black pudding or white pudding – fried slices of blood or barley sausage. This is usually accompanied by homemade, crumbly soda bread, large portions of salted butter and as much tea and milk as can be drunk (coffee, though it is available everywhere, is often of the instant variety).

Traditional Irish cuisine is heavily reliant on the potato, along with smaller amounts of pork, mutton or beef and vegetables. Meat consumption is not that high, apart from sausages, ham and bacon. Many age-old recipes (or modern ones pretending to be age-old) feature corned beef, which is cooked with nutmeg, cinnamon and other spices in wintertime to create spiced beef. The world-famous Irish stew is really just a collective term for all kinds of recipes based on the meat-and-vegetable hotpot. In the north of Ireland the stew is composed of mutton, potatoes and onions. In the south they add carrots as well, and some fanatics from Tipperary even insist that mutton in a stew should be replaced by beef.

Dairy products are enjoyed in massive quantities (the Irish drink more milk than any other country in the EU), but relatively little seafood is eaten (half as much per head as the Spanish). For an island in the Atlantic with the reputation of being a paradise for anglers, this is perverse. But the variety of fish is a mainstay of haute cuisine – oys-

Pub Life
A trip to the pub in Ireland is not just for a piss-up (getting drunk) but seen as the place to have a good ol' chin wag (chat) along with a pint of stout (Guinness) and good craic (a good time). Whiskey meant water of life in Gaelic and the pubs are the hubs around which Irish life entertainingly turns.

ters and lobster from the West Coast, and Irish salmon are world-famous.

Although all the usual international soft drinks can be found in Ireland, along with local mineral water and the normal range of alcoholic beverages, two drinks tend to predominate: whiskey and stout. The product of Dublin's Guinness brewery is well-known everywhere, of course, but anyone who gets a chance should test the competition: Murphy's, for instance, from Cork, which contains less hops and is therefore not as bitter, or Beamish which many people say tastes the way Guinness once used to. Whiskey in Ireland is part of an old, long-standing tradition – the Bushmills distillery in Northern Ireland received its first licence in 1608. Irish whiskey differs from the Scots version by being distilled three times rather than twice; by often being produced in pot stills, which makes it gentler; and by being spelled with an 'e'. The malt is also not exposed to smoke during roasting. Delicious *Power's*, with its high pot-still distillate content and unmashed malt, can be found in every pub in the Republic.

Restaurant selection

Here is a list of some restaurants in Ireland. €€€ means expensive, €€ medium-priced and € inexpensive. Pubs are also appended.

> **Tourist Taste**
> Thanks to the tourist trade, several long-neglected recipes are now being offered once again such as Crubeens (pigs' trotters), Drisheen (a black pudding made with sheep's blood), Barm Brack (a sweet fruit bread), Colcannon (a traditional Lent dish containing cabbage, milk, butter and onions) and Carrageen Pudding (a sweet milk pudding, sometimes vanilla-flavoured, in which the milk has been thickened with seaweed).

Ardara
Nesbitt Arms, tel: 074-954 1103. Friendly pub serving excellent food. €

Baltimore
Chez Youen (at the harbour), tel: 028-20136, www.youenjacob.com. Breton cuisine, delicious and artistically served. €€
Rolf's, tel: 028-20289, www.rolfsholidays. com. Rustic, family-run informal restaurant on a hill overlooking the bay.

Belfast
Deane's, 36–40 Howard Street, tel: 028-9033 1134, www.deanesbelfast.com. Classic cuisine from one of Ireland's finest chefs. €€€ Informal brasserie (€€) on ground floor.
Cayenne, 7 Ascot House, Shaftesbury Square, tel: 028-9033 1532, www.cayenne restaurant.com. The hippest place in town, offering a light fusion menu. €€
Harry Ramsden's, Yorkgate Complex, 150a York Street, tel: 028-9074 9222. World-famous fish and chips served in traditional environment. €€
Café Paul Rankin, 27–29 Fountain Street, tel: 028-9031 5090. Informal, day-time eaterie run by TV chefs Paul and Jeanne Rankin of Cayenne. €
Crown Liquor Saloon, 46 Great Victoria Street, tel: 028-9024 9476. Symphony in tile and mirror; cosy snugs.
Fountain Tavern, 16 Fountain Street. One of Belfast's oldest pubs and one of its most welcoming.
Kitchen Bar, 16–18 Victoria Square. Traditional bar dates back to 1859.
White's Tavern, 2–4 Winecellar Entry. Dates to 1630 and set in a narrow cobbled lane: tradition at its finest.

Clifden
The Signal Restaurant, Station House, tel: 095-22946. The Swiss brothers Matz give local produce an imaginative, contemporary twist. €€€
Mitchell's, Market Street, tel: 095-212867, Busy town centre restaurant

offering Irish stew, local seafood and bacon and cabbage plus international fare on day and evening menus. €

Cork

Ivory Tower, Exchange Buildings, Princes Street, tel: 021-427 4665. Mildly eccentric home base of Seamus O'Connell, TV cook (Soul Food), and one of Ireland's most creative chefs. €€
Jacob's on the Mall, South Mall, tel: 021-425 1530. Stylish European cooking in a former Turkish baths. €€
Proby's Bistro, Crosses Green, tel: 021-431 6531, www.probysbistro.com. Large bistro serving Mediterranean cuisines. €€
Crawford Gallery Café, Municipal Art Gallery, tel: 021-427 4415. Excellent but often crowded. €
Quay Co-Op, 24 Sullivan's Quay, tel: 021-431 7660, www.quaycoop.com. Good vegetarian food. €
An Spailpín Fánac, 28/29 South Main Opposite Beamish Brewery with live music during the evenings.
The Lobby/Charlie's/An Ears. Three pubs along Union Quay south of the Lee. A good place for music.

Derry

Brown's, 1–2 Bond Hill, tel: 028-7134 5180, www.brownsrestaurant.com. Choose from restaurant, bar or brasserie at the city's leading restaurant. €€
McGilloways Seafood Restaurant, 145 Strand Road, tel: 028-71 262 050. Fresh local fish prepared by creative chef. Interior based on old-fashioned chip shop. €€
Dungloe, 41 Waterloo Street. Young clientele, folk/blues/rock.
O'Donnell's, 63 Waterloo Street. Old-fashioned pub.

Dingle

Doyle's, 4 John Street, tel: 066-915 1174, www.doylesofdingle.com. Justly renowned and long-established seafood restaurant. €€€

Dublin

Locks, 1 Windsor Terrace, tel: 01-454 3391. First-class French and Irish cuisine with friendly atmosphere, justly recommended by many guides. €€€
Elephant & Castle, 18 Temple Bar, tel: 01-679 3121. More New York-Irish than Dublin-Irish, serves oversized salads and burgers. €
O'Donoghue's, 15 Merrion Row. Dublin's best pub for live folk music.
The Brazen Head, Lower Bridge Street, www.brazenhead.com. It claims to be Dublin's oldest pub.
Mulligan's, 8 Poolbeg Street, tel: 01-677 5582. Reputedly serves the best Guinness in Dublin.

Enniskillen

Killyhevlin Hotel, Dublin Road, tel: 028-632 481, www.killyhevlin.com. On the banks of Lough Erne, 1km (½ mile) from Enniskillen. Buffet lunch and good evening meals. €€

Galway

MacDonagh's, Quay Street, tel: 091-565 001. Brilliant fish whether baked, fried or served next to tasty oysters. €€
Nimmo's, The Long Walk, Spanish Arch, tel: 091-563 565. Imaginative continental-style cuisine in romantic riverside stone building. €€
Malt House, Olde Malte Arcade, High Street, tel: 091-563 993. Steaks and seafood in old world atmosphere of town centre pub-restaurant. €–€€
O'Neachtain's, Quay Street. Friendly bar, folk music, with restaurant.

Howth

King Sitric, East Pier, Harbour Road, tel: 01-832 5235, www.kingsitric.com. Exquisite fish. €€€

Kilkenny

Lacken House, Dublin Road, tel: 056-776 1085, www.lackenhouse.ie. Much-praised Irish cuisine. €€

Langton's, 69 John Street, tel: 056-776 5133. Prizewinning pub with separate restaurant. €

Caisleán Ui Cuain, 2 High Street. Friendly and cosy pub.

Killarney

Foley's Town House, 23 High Street, tel: 064-31217. Steak and seafood. €€

The Old Presbytery, Cathedral Place, tel: 064-30557, www.oldpresbytery.com. Fine dining and friendly staff in spacious, stylishly converted historic house. €€

Kinsale

Blue Haven, 3 Pearse Street, tel: 021-477 2209, www.bluehavenkinsale.com. Probably the best restaurant in town. €€

Crackpots, 3 Cork Street, tel: 021-477 2847, www.crackpots.ie. Eclectic menu with unusual vegetarian options in a cosy, cottage-style setting. €€

Mullingar

Crookedwood House, Crookedwood (on the R394, 10km/6 miles north of Mullingar), tel: 044-72165, www.crookedwoodhouse.com. Praiseworthy Irish cuisine. Set in a 200-year-old manse on the banks of a lough. €€

Portrush

Ramore, Portrush, The Harbour, tel: 028-70824313, www.portrushharbour.co.uk. Justly praised in many food guides, great value. €€

Harbour Bar, Portrush, www.portrushharbour.co.uk. This is an institution. The Guinness is excellent.

Portstewart

Smyths Restaurant, 2 Lever Road, tel: 028-7083 3564. French style and Irish hospitality in a traditional family home. Features fresh seafood. €€

Shanagarry

Ballymaloe House, tel: 021-465 2531, www.ballymaloe.ie. Myrtle Allen led the revival in Irish cuisine here using fresh produce from the farm, and the younger generations carry on the tradition at the famous country-house hotel. Book well in advance. €€€

Sligo

McGettigan's, Connolly Street, tel: 071-917 0933. Comfortable bar, good food. €€

D McLynn's, Old Market Street. A popular pub for folk music.

Waterford

The Wine Vault, High Street, tel: 051-853 444, www.waterfordwinevault.com. Located in an 18th-century warehouse beneath a 15th-century tower house, wine is a strong point at this busy, cheerful venue. €–€€

Haricot's Wholefood, 11 O'Connell Street. Vegetarian food and delicious home-made ice cream. €

Henry Downes, 10 Thomas Street. The pub has its very own whiskey – Henry Downes No 9.

Westport

Asgard Tavern, the Quay. Cosy bar with good food near the harbour. €

Matt Molloy's Bar, Bridge Street. Owned by *the* Matt Molloy, flute-player with *The Chieftains* – so traditional music is very important here.

Wexford

Forde's, Crescent Quay, tel: 053-22 816. Owner-chef offers eclectic menu with seafood emphasis in first floor bistro overlooking the harbour. €€

Thomas Moore Tavern, Cornmarket, nice and quiet, inside an old building.

Tower Bar, Commercial Quay, regular live music.

Youghal

Aherne's Seafood Restaurant, 163 Main Street, tel: 024-92424, www.ahernes.com. Prizewinning s seafood. €€

ACTIVE HOLIDAYS

Ireland is very well equipped for the active holidaymaker, and the two tourist authorities – Tourism Ireland/ Fáilte Ireland in Eire (www.ireland.ie) and the Northern Irish Tourist Board (www.discovernorthernireland.com) – supply all kinds of brochures listing prices and contact addresses for all manner of activities. Many of these, such as angling, boating, riding and golf, are a lot cheaper if booked as part of a package that includes a return fare, rather than directly from the organisers in Ireland.

ANGLING

Ireland provides some of the best fishing in Europe; the Republic's salmon, sea trout and freshwater trout seasons (15 February until 12 October) are both long, even though the pickings aren't consistently good. The best time for salmon is the end of March, for sea trout from the end of May, and for freshwater trout April to June and also September. For trout and salmon fishing a state permit is required; it costs 30 euros for the season, 15 euros for 21 days or 8 euros a day, from all tackle shops or from the offices of the Fisheries Board. For more information contact the Central Fisheries Board, Balnagowan House, Mobhi Boreen, Glasnevin, Dublin 9, tel: 01-837 9206, fax: 836 0060. Permits for particular waters cost between 7 and 90 euros a day for sea trout and salmon. Other freshwater fishing and sea angling grounds are free of charge (see www.cfb.ie).

CABIN CRUISERS

The majestic Shannon river and its large lakes, Lough Derg (www.loughderg. org) and Lough Ree (www.loughree.com), form the largest and most popular fishing ground, while the lake area of Upper and Lower Lough Earne in Fermanagh in Northern Ireland is quieter and perhaps even more attractive. Since the re-opening of the 62-km (38-mile) Shannon-Erne Waterway across the border, boat-trippers have practically the whole of central Ireland at their disposal.

CYCLING

Another peaceful and healthy way of appreciating Ireland is to go on a cycling holiday (bike tours around the

Canoeing in County Galway

Dingle Peninsula and the Ring of Kerry are particularly popular). Raleigh Ireland (www.raleigh.ie) has rental outlets all over the Republic; for more information contact its head office at Raleigh House, Kylemore Road, Dublin 10, tel: 01-626 1333, fax: 626 1770. There are also other local firms that do the same.

Organised tours with luggage transport and pre-booked accommodation are increasingly popular. Contact Irish Cycling Safaris, Belfield House, University College, Dublin 4, tel: 01-260 0749, www.cyclingsafaris.com.

For more information on cycling in Northern Ireland go to www.nationalcycle network.co.uk.

GOLF

Ireland has around 300 magnificent golf courses, most of them open to non-members. Some of the courses out in open countryside, known as 'links', by the sea are among the most famous in Europe. Alongside the usual tourist office brochures more information can be obtained from the Golfing Union of Ireland, 81 Eglinton Road, Dublin 4, tel: 01-269 4111, fax: 269 5368, www.gui.ie.

HIKING

The longest of Ireland's hiking routes is the Ulster Way, which leads around 700km (430 miles) through the whole

> **Pub Crawling**
> It should also be mentioned that Ireland's great literary tradition has its own special activity too. Try the 'Dublin Literary Pub Crawl', a very Irish invention. Two actors take those interested on a two-hour tour of Dublin's pubs, reciting, singing and telling anecdotes from the lives of famous Irish authors who used to frequent the same establishments: Joyce, Beckett, Yeats and many more.

of Northern Ireland. The most attractive scenery to hike through is up in the Mountains of Mourne in the northeast, MacGillicuddy's Reeks in the southwest, or Mount Brandon on the Dingle Peninsula – elsewhere it's hard to avoid the motor traffic. Some companies offer guided walking trails such as Sperrin Trails. See www.sperrintrails.com for more details.

Clonmel in County Tipperary makes a great base for exploring the Comeragh or Knockmealdown Mountains as well as Slievenamon.

HORSE-DRAWN CARTS AND CARAVANS

Holidaying in a horse-drawn caravan has been an Irish speciality for many years now. All you do is cross the countryside in the company of a good-natured horse which pulls a simple, yet comfortably furnished caravan behind it. Caravans and carts can be rented in Kerry, Laois and Wicklow – Fáilte Ireland (www.ireland.ie) can provide all the addresses.

HORSE-RIDING

The Irish appear to have a remarkable affinity with horses, and riding holidays here can be particularly enjoyable. Stabling, tuition, day rides or tours are provided all over the country, especially in the counties of Wicklow and Meath, and also County Cork (see www.horseireland.com).

WATER SPORTS AND SAILING

Ireland's 5,600km (3,470 miles) of coastline, 14,000km (8,600 miles) of rivers and 4,000 lakes make it a water sports paradise. Coastal waters and loughs are fine for swimming, yachting and windsurfing. Further information from the Irish Sailing Association, 3 Park Road, Dun Laoghaire, Co. Dublin, tel: 01-280 0239, fax: 280 7558, www.sailing.ie.

PRACTICAL INFORMATION

Getting There

BY AIR

Dublin airport (www.dublin-airport.com) handles flights from Europe whilst transatlantic flights arrive at Shannon airport. There are frequent flights to both airports and considerable competition between the airlines, including the Irish carriers Aer Lingus and Ryanair. It is well worth shopping around for low-cost fares and fly/drive packages.

Aer Lingus (tel: 0845-9737 747, www.aerlingus.com) serves Dublin, Cork, Galway, Kerry, Shannon and Sligo. Its Irish flights connect with Boston, New York, London Heathrow, Manchester, Edinburgh, Paris, Dusseldorf and Frankfurt.

Manx Airlines (tel: 0845-256 256, www.manx-airlines.com) flies from London and Luton to Waterford and the new Kerry Airport, serving Ireland's southeast and southwest respectively.

Competitive prices are available on all UK–Ireland routes. Virgin (tel: 01293-747 747, www.virgin-atlantic.com) offers a smooth flight from London City Airport to Dublin, matched by bmi British Midland (tel: 0870-6070 555, www.flybmi.com) flights from London Heathrow and British Airways (tel: 08457-66 44 55, www.britishairways.com) flights from London Gatwick. Ryanair (tel: 08701-569 569, www.ryanair.com) offers good economy flights from London Stansted to Dublin, Knock and Cork. From Dublin, the Airlink bus connects with the city centre, bus and rail stations.

There are flights from most main British airports, as well as Paris and Amsterdam, to Belfast International Airport (www.bial.co.uk) at Aldergrove in Northern Ireland (tel: 028-94484848); there are frequent services between Aldergrove and London's Heathrow.

Belfast City Airport (tel: 028-9093 9093, www.belfastcityairport.com), 6km (4 miles) from the city centre, handles domestic flights to Scotland and England.

BY SEA

Irish Ferries (tel: 08705-170000, www.irishferries.ie) runs services between the UK port of Holyhead on the Isle of Anglesea and Dublin North Wall, and also between Pembroke and Rosslare, on the southeast coast. Stena Line (tel: 08705-707070, www.stenaline.co.uk) operates between Holyhead and Dun Laoghaire, just south of Dublin and between Fishguard and Rosslare. Irish Ferries also offer three sailings a week between Rosslare and the French ports of Le Havre and Cherbourg (tel: Rosslare 053-33158 or Dublin 01-661 0511).

For Northern Ireland, Stena Line (tel: 08705-204204, www.stenaline.co.uk) operates a service from Stranraer in Scotland to Belfast, the same route plied by the faster SeaCat Scotland service (tel: 08705-523 523). P&O Ferries (tel: 08705-980980, www.poscottishferries.com) runs between Cairnryan in Scotland and Larne, and Norse Irish Ferries (tel: 0870-600 4321, www.norsemerchant.com) between Liverpool and Belfast. Belfast is also served from the Isle of Man by Douglas Isle of Man Steam Packet (tel: 01624-661661, www.steam-packet.com).

Getting Around

BY RAIL

The main railway lines in Ireland spread out in a fan shape from Dublin, and the western part of Northern Ireland and the southernmost part of the Republic are both badly connected. The lack of cross-routes

> ### Dublin Transport
> Dublin's transportation system relies heavily upon its double decker buses with considerable help from the DART rail system (www.irishrail.ie/dart) for reaching the extended suburbs. Dublin Bus (www.dublinbus.ie) operates an extensive network of buses throughout the city. A less comprehensive network of Nitelink buses run into the wee hours. All buses require correct change so be prepared. The new LUAS tram system has two routes, one of which crosses the city centre connecting Heuston and Connolly rail stations.

means that very large detours sometimes have to be made just to travel north-south in the west of Ireland, e.g. getting from Galway to Sligo, a distance of just 130km (80 miles) involves taking a rail journey (plus changing) of 280km (173 miles). Contact Irish Rail (www.irishrail.ie) for times and destinations: 1850 366 222 in Ireland and 353 183 662 22 outside the country.

BY BUS

In contrast, the long-distance bus routes in Northern Ireland (Ulsterbus) and the Republic (Bus Éireann) are well developed (see www.buseireann.ie). In summer, extra bus routes are provided, especially on the west coast, and travel costs are around half as much as the equivalent trip by train, though the journey can often take longer. Combination tickets are not cheap, but they do allow optimal use of the public transport system: the Emerald Card ticket, for instance, is valid on trains and long-distance buses in both Northern Ireland and the Republic for 8 journeys of any desired length within 15 calendar days.

BY CAR

The Irish drive on the left, like the English, and the highway code is very much the same too. Cars on round-abouts have priority, otherwise the theoretical system of 'right before left' applies. The speed limits are 30mph (48kmph) in built-up areas, 60mph (96kmph) on country roads and 70mph (113kmph) on motorways and dual carriageways. Plans are under way to convert all speed limits and road signs to kilometres per hour in 2005. Ask on arrival.

In Northern Ireland all distances are given in miles. In the Republic, speed limits are always given in miles and so are the distances on the old white roadsigns, but the new white signs and all the green signs show the distances in kilometres (with *km* above the number). All place names are in English and Gaelic, so if you reach a sign to Dublin and Baile Atha Cliath (abbreviated to Atha Cliath on some signs), don't bother deciding which one you want to head for – they're one and the same place. In the *Gaeltacht* (*see page 12*) signs are only in Gaelic.

BY AIR

The Aran Islands off Galway Bay can be comfortably reached by plane as well as by ferry. Flights are from Connemara Airport at Inverin with Aer Árann, tel: 091-568903, fax: 593238, www.aerarann.ie, flight time is 8–10 minutes, and there are charter connections to all three islands.

Facts for the Visitor

CUSTOMS

Goods from countries in the EU destined for personal use can be taken freely in and out of Ireland by EU citizens. The following allowances apply solely to goods from non-EU countries or travellers from EU countries: 200 cigarettes or 250g tobacco, 1l alcoholic beverages above 22 percent or 2l alcohol below 22 percent, 60ml perfume or 250ml eau de toilette.

TOURIST INFORMATION

Northern Ireland is represented by the Northern Ireland Tourist Board (www.discovernorthernireland.com) and the Republic by Tourism Ireland/Fáilte Ireland (www.ireland.ie).

In the UK: *Northern Ireland Tourist Board*, Britain Visitor Centre, 1 Lower Regent Street, London, tel: 0870-1555 250 (brochures). *Tourism Ireland*, Nations House, 103 Wigmore Street, London W1U 1QS, tel: 020-7518 0800, fax: 020-7493 9065.
In the US: *Northern Ireland Tourist Board*, 551 Fifth Avenue, Suite 701, New York, NY 10176, tel: 212-922 0101, fax: 212-922 0099. *Tourism Ireland*, 345 Park Avenue, New York, NY 10154, tel: 212-418 0800, fax: 212-371 9052.
In Ireland: *Northern Ireland Tourist Board*, 59 North Street, Belfast BT1 1NB, tel: 028-9024 6609, fax: 028-9031 2424; 16 Nassau Street, Dublin 2, tel: 01-679 1977, fax: 01-679 1863. *Tourism Ireland*, 53 Castle Street, Belfast, tel: 028-90327888; Baggot Street Bridge, Dublin, tel: 01-602 4000, fax: 602 4100. *Dublin Tourism*, Suffolk Street, Dublin 2, www.visitdublin.com.

Most towns have a tourist information office (Republic), or a tourist information centre (Northern Ireland), usually open weekdays 10am–5pm. Those in larger towns often stay open into the evening and at the weekend.

CURRENCY AND EXCHANGE

The official unit of currency in the Republic of Ireland is the euro (€). Notes are denominated in 5, 10, 20, 50, 100 and 500 euros; coins in 1 and 2 euros and 1, 2, 5, 10, 20 and 50 cents.

In Northern Ireland, the unit of currency is the English pound sterling (£), made up of 100 pence (p). There are 1, 2, 5, 10, 20, 50p and £1 coins, and

Dublin explorer
Unlimited travel on Dublin Bus, DART and suburban rail services for four consecutive days costs around 13 euros.

5, 10, 20 and £50 notes. Traveller's cheques and eurocheques can be cashed at any bank without a problem, and a lot of bank machines accept credit/debit cards. Credit cards are accepted almost everywhere.

English currency is usually happily accepted in the Republic and the euro is accepted at many outlets in Northern Ireland.

OPENING TIMES

Banks: As a rule, Monday–Friday 10am–12.30pm and 1.30–3pm, in Dublin until 5pm on Thursday, in Northern Ireland 9.30am–3.30pm.

Shops: Usually Monday to Saturday 10am–5.30pm, and often open late into the evening and at the weekend during peak season. Early closing day, when country shops close at noon, is normally Wednesday or Thursday.

Pubs: In the Republic Monday–Saturday 10.30am–11.30pm, Sunday 12.30–2pm and 4–11pm; in Northern Ireland 11am–11pm, though some pubs choose to have shorter opening hours on Sunday.

Post offices: In the Republic, Monday to Friday 9am–6pm (often closed for lunch in country areas) and Saturday 9am–noon; in Northern Ireland Monday to Friday 9am–5.30pm, Saturday 9am–12.30pm.

Opening times for museums, sights, etc tend to be changed without much notice; check first with local tourist information.

Public Holidays

New Year's Day, 17 March (St Patrick's Day – Republic only), Good Friday, Easter Monday, 12 July (Orange Day – Northern Ireland only), Christmas Day and Boxing Day. There are also three bank holidays: the first Monday in May, the last Monday in May, and the first Monday in August (Northern Ireland) or the first Monday in June, and the last Monday in October (Republic).

Wired Land

You'll have little problem getting on line in Ireland. In all major cities, Internet cafés are invading the high streets, especially in the vicinity of tourist offices.

Telephoning

Coin-operated phones take 10, 20 and 50 cent pieces and also euro coins. Phonecards are sold at post offices and many shops.

To telephone the Republic from Great Britain or Northern Ireland, first dial 00353. To call the UK from the Republic, first dial 0044. To call Northern Ireland from the UK call 028 (44-28 from outside the UK; or 048 from Eire).

Time

The whole of Ireland is on Greenwich Mean Time (GMT), i.e. the same as England, which is 5 hours ahead of Eastern Standard Time in the United States and usually one hour behind continental Europe.

Tipping

Taxi drivers expect 10 to 15 percent on top of the fare, and so do hairdressers and waiters in restaurants wherever menus say 'service not included'. Bar staff in pubs are not tipped as a rule.

Voltage

The voltage in Ireland is 220 volts AC. Hotels usually have dual 220/110 voltage sockets for electric razors only. To use their own small appliances, visitors may need a plug adaptor to fit Ireland's 3-pin flat or 2-pin round sockets.

Disabled

Detailed brochures are available from Fáilte Ireland in the Republic *(Accommodations for the Disabled)* and from the Northern Irish Tourist Board *(The Disabled Tourist in Northern Ireland)*. Further information can also be obtained from the *National Disability Resource Centre*, 44 North Great George's Street, Dublin 1, tel: 01-874 7503.

Emergencies

For fire, police or ambulance assistance, the number to dial all over Ireland is 999.

Medical assistance

For visitors from the United Kingdom, Northern Ireland provides the same free treatment on the NHS as other parts of the UK. In the Republic, visitors from the UK need only show some proof of identity. Visitors from other EU countries are entitled to medical treatment throughout Ireland, North and South, under a reciprocal arrangement, but should carry form E111, available in their own country. All other travellers should take out medical insurance.

Diplomatic representation

British Embassy, 31 Merrion Rd, Dublin 4, tel: 01-269 5211, www.britishembassy.ie. United States Embassy, 42 Elgin Rd, Dublin 4, tel: 01-688777, www.usembassy.ie. American Consulate General, Queen's Street, Belfast, tel: 028-9032 8329, www.usembassy.org.uk.

ACCOMMODATION

One reads now and then that accommodation in Ireland is never really bad. Although that shouldn't be taken literally (over-expensive or dismal-looking establishments should certainly be avoided), the fact is that hardly any visitors complain about an unfriendly reception or dirty rooms. Fáilte Ireland, the Republic's tourist authority, and the Northern Ireland Tourist Board north of the border have been doing their best to secure a good reputation for tourism, a vital component of the economy. Both organisations are generally helpful and informative when it comes to finding somewhere to stay (they have offices in nearly every town) and can provide a great deal of printed information on almost any topic, including the hotels' own reference guide *Hotels & Guesthouses – Be Our Guest* (www.ireland hotels.com). More detailed (and more objective) information can be found in *The Bridgestone 100 Best Places to Stay in Ireland* and Georgina Campbell's *Jameson Guide*.

Holiday houses are becoming increasingly popular, from the self-catering bungalow to the beautifully situated country cottage. More information can be obtained from the *Guide to Self-Catering Accommodation*, available from Fáilte Ireland.

HOTELS

Tourism has boomed in Ireland over the past 30 years or so, and there are numerous modern hotels. Pleasant additions like saunas and indoor swimming pools sometimes can't make up for ugly architecture and sterile furnishings. Living in a hotel in Ireland isn't cheap, but those who can afford luxury or who want to splash out will find a magnificent range of country houses and castles, some of which are described in the *Places* section.

BED & BREAKFAST

There are bed and breakfast establishments all over the place; most of those in the Republic have a green sign outside with a shamrock showing that they are subject to regular inspection by the Fáilte Ireland. A hot evening meal is often provided too. A stay at a B&B proves that the Irish really are a hospitable people. The disadvantage of a longer stay, however, is that you're expected to leave the house during the

House hotels offer comfort – at a price

day, and after a week in the same place in bad weather this can get rather frustrating. In this respect, guesthouses and hotels are more comfortable (though the room may be less so).

HOTEL SELECTION

Here is a list of some hotels, guesthouses and B&B establishments. €€€ = expensive, €€ = medium-priced and € = inexpensive.

Ardara

The Green Gate, tel: 075-954 1546. A night at this B&B has to be one of the best experiences in Ireland. Perched high atop a coastal mountain, Atlantic winds sing you to sleep and the ocean waits outside your window come morning. €

Athlone

Hodson Bay Hotel, Roscommon Road, tel: 090-644 2000, www.hodsonbay hotel.com. Located on the shore of Lough Ree with breathtaking views. €€

Ballymacarbry

Hanorah's Cottage, Nire Valley, tel: 052-36134, fax: 36540, www.hanoras cottage.com. Hikers in Waterford's Comeragh mountains appreciate the comfort of this award-winning riverside retreat. €€

Bantry

Atlanta House, Main Street, tel: 027-50237, www.atlantaguesthouse.com. Family run guesthouse makes a great base to tour west Cork. €

Belfast

Hastings Europa Hotel, Great Victoria Street, tel: 028-9027 1066, www.hastingshotels.com. Cosmopolitan and world-famous four-star hotel across the road from the famous Crown Liquor Saloon. Ensuite rooms with satellite TV and movies. €€€

The Crescent Townhouse, 13 Lower Crescent, tel: 028-9032 3349, fax: 9032 0646, www.crescenttownhouse.com. A short stroll from both the university and the city centre, the spacious, country-style rooms are above a lively brasserie. €€
Dukes Hotel, 65 University Street, tel: 028-9023 6666, www.welcome-group.co.uk. Modern hotel with Victorian facade. €€
The Old Rectory, 148 Malone Road, tel: 028-9066 7882, e-mail: info@ anoldrectory.co.uk. Once a Church of Ireland rectory, this guest house now serves an overwhelming breakfast and provides free hot whiskey at night. €€
Queen's Elm's Halls of Residence, 78 Malone Road, tel: 028-9038 1608. Self-catering rooms available during university holidays. €

Cashel

Cashel Palace Hotel, Main Street, tel: 062-62707, www.cashel-palace.ie. Former episcopal palace built in 1730 with a view of the Rock. €€€

Cashel Bay

Cashel House, tel: 095-31001, fax: 31077, www.cashel-house-hotel.com. Luxury hotel with a famous restaurant. €€€
Zetland House, tel: 095-31111, fax: 31117, www.zetland.com. Situated on a small rise with a good view. €€€

Campsites

These are numerous in the popular tourist areas, but rather rare in others. Lists can be obtained from the Fáilte Ireland and the NITB. Commercial campsites are usually well equipped with modern conveniences, but they are no cheaper than hostels and hardly any cheaper than the modest variety of B&Bs either, breakfast included. In the old days 'camping out' was normal across the whole country, and farmers will usually let you camp on their land if you ask politely – sometimes for a small fee.

Clifden

Abbeyglen Castle Hotel, Sky Road, tel: 095-22832, fax: 21797, www.abbeyglen.ie. A pleasant hotel in a weird-looking concrete house built in the 1930s for a wealthy gentleman racing driver. €€

The Quay House, Beach Road, tel: 095-21369, www.thequayhouse.com. Comfortable rooms. €€

Cork

Imperial Hotel, South Mall, tel: 021-427 4040, fax: 427 5375, www.imperialhotelcork.ie. Traditional city hotel, centrally located, grandiose foyer. €€€

Ambassador Hotel, Military Hill, St Lukes, tel: 021-455 1996, fax: 455 1997, www.ambassadorhotel.ie. A red brick Victorian nursing home has been converted into a stylish, hill top hotel with great views of the harbour. €€

Victoria Hotel Patrick Street, tel: 021 427 8788, www.thevictoriahotel.com. Mentioned in Joyce's *Portrait of the Artist as a Young Man* and visited by royalty. The Vic Bar is equally classic. €€

Lotamore House, Tivoli (near Lower Glanmire Road), tel: 021-482 2344, fax: 482 2219, e-mail: lotamore@iol.ie. Good value in large period house on edge of city. €

Derry

Beech Hill Country House, 32 Ardmore Road (in Ardmore, 5km/3 miles southeast of the town centre), tel: 028-7134 4927, fax: 7134 5366. Well-appointed rooms, country house with its own park, great food too. €€€

Joan Pyne, 36 Great James Street (Bogside, north of the old town), tel: 028-7126 9691, fax: 7126 6913, www.thesaddlershouse.com. Much praised B&B establishment. €

Donegal

Harvey's Point Country Hotel, Lough Eske (10km/6 miles northeast of Donegal, follow signs from the N15 to Harvey's Point and Ardnamona), tel: 073-22208, fax: 22352, www.harveyspoint.com. Comfortable hotel in a Victorian hunting lodge with a famous rhododendron garden. €€€

Dublin

Clarence, 6–8 Wellington Quay, tel: 01-407 0800, fax: 407 0820, www.theclarence.ie. U2's stylish Temple Bar hotel. Great restaurant. €€€

Georgian Hotel, 18/22 Lower Baggot Street, tel: 01-634 5000, fax: 634 5100, e-mail: info@georgianhotel.ie. Good hotel in 18th-century townhouse. €€€

Shelbourne Hotel, 27 St Stephen's Green, tel: 01-663 4500, fax: 661 6006, www.shelbourne.ie. Dublin's most prestigious hotel. €€€

Trinity Lodge 12 South Frederick Street, tel: 01-679 5044, fax: 679 5223, www.trinitylodge.com. Ideally situated for visiting Temple Bar, Trinity College and Grafton Street. Rooms are spacious and elegant. €€€

Staunton's on the Green, 83 St Stephen's Green, tel: 01-478 2300, fax: 478 2263, www.stauntonsonthegreen.ie. Well situated, elegant guest house. €€

Bewleys' Ballsbridge, Merrion Road, tel: 01-668 1111, fax: 668 1999, www.bewleyshotels.com. In a leafy location next to the RDS exhibition centre, a short bus ride from town, this landmark period building is now a large, bustling hotel. €

Enniskillen

Killyhevlin Hotel, Killyhevlin, tel: 028-6632 3481, fax: 6632 4726, www.killyhevlin.com. Modern hotel on the shore of Lough Erne. €€

Galway

Ardilaun House, Taylor's Hill, tel: 091-521433, fax: 521546, www.ardilaunhousehotel.ie. Large country house built in 1840, quiet location south of city centre. €€€

Great Southern Hotel, Eyre Square, tel: 091-564041, fax: 566704, www.gshotels.com. Large and elegant hotel. **€€€**

Skeffington Arms Hotel, 28 Eyre Square, tel: 091-563 173, fax: 561 679, www.skeffington.ie. A small hotel in the centre of Galway, family-run and friendly. The bar and leading night club will keep you entertained. **€€**

Corrib Haven, 107 Upper Newcastle, tel: 091-524 171, fax: 582 414, www.corribhaven.com. This luxurious B&B on the N59 Connemara road is a good touring base, and also convenient to the city centre. **€**

Kenmare

Park Hotel, tel: 064-41200, fax: 41402, www.parkkenmare.com. A top luxury hotel and spa. **€€€**

Sheen Falls Lodge, tel: 064-41600, fax: 41386, www.sheenfallslodge.ie. Only 3km/1 mile from the Park Hotel, also luxurious. **€€€**

Kilkenny

Mount Juliet Conrad, Thomastown (18km/11 miles south of Kilkenny), tel: 056-777 3000, fax: 777 3019, www.mountjulietconrad.com. An 18th-century country house with riding facilities, a golf course, fishing, hunting, almost too expensive to relax in properly. **€€€**

Butler's House, Patrick Street, tel: 056-772 2828, fax: 776 5626, www.butler.ie. A Georgian town house with beautiful spacious rooms overlooking the river and stunning gardens leading to the Kilkenny Design Centre. **€€**

Club House Hotel, Patrick Street, tel: 056-772 1994, fax: 777 1920, www.clubhousehotel.com. Centrally located and comfortable. **€€**

Kilford Arms, John Street, tel: 056-776 1018, fax: 776 1128, www.kilfordarms.ie. Set above a traditional pub, trendy nightclub and stylish late bar. Smart rooms and located in the city centre. Exciting atmosphere. **€€**

Killarney

Foley's Town House, 23 High Street, tel: 064-31217. Comfortable rooms, good for families with children. **€€**

Lake Hotel, Muckross Road, tel: 064-31035, fax: 31902, www.lakehotel.com. Characterful long-established hotel with a prime lakeshore location. **€€**

Kinsale

Blue Haven, 3 Pearse Street, tel: 021-477 2209, fax: 477 4268, www.bluehavenkinsale.com. Considered by many to be the best place to stay (and eat) in town. **€€€**

Old Presbytery, Cork Street, tel: 021-477 2027, fax: 477 2166, www.oldpres.com. Old world luxury in town centre. **€€€**

Friar's Lodge, Friar Street, tel: 021-477 3445, fax: 477 4363, www.friars-lodge.com. Sumptuously converted Georgian townhouse with large rooms offering excellent value bed and breakfast. **€**

Lisdoonvarna

Sheedy's Spa View Hotel, tel: 065-707 4026, fax: 707 4555, www.sheedys.com. Family-owned for generations, comfortable rooms and a good restaurant too. **€€**

Oughterard

Sweeney's Oughterard House, tel: 091-552207, fax: 552161, e-mail: phiggins@iol.ie. Country house hotel with slightly faded old-world charm. **€€**

Portrush

Magherabuoy House Hotel, 41 Magherabuoy Road, Portrush, tel: 028-7082 3507, fax: 7082 4687, www.magherabuoy.co.uk. Comfortable hotel on a hill above the town centre. **€€**

Rathmullan

Rathmullan House, tel: 074-915 8188, fax: 915 8200, www.rathmullanhouse.com. The best hotel for miles around, with rooms ranging from simple to luxurious. **€€€**

Rathnew

Hunter's Hotel, Newrath Bridge, tel: 0404-40106, fax: 40338, www.hunters.ie. This romantic hideaway is one of Ireland's oldest coaching inns with an excellent restaurant and award-winning gardens. €€

Shanagarry

Ballymaloe House, tel: 021-465 2531, fax: 465 2021, www.ballmaloe.ie. One of the most famous hotels in the Republic, very comfortable, with cookery school nearby and restaurant attached, excellent for families, 40 minutes' drive from Cork. €€€

Sligo

Ballincar House Hotel, Rosses Point Road (roughly 3km/a mile north of town centre), tel: 071-45361, fax: 44198. Not exciting but quiet and clean, with a decent restaurant. €€€
Clarence Hotel, Wine Street, tel: 071- 42211. Centrally located and cheap. €€

Westport

Olde Railway Hotel, The North Mall, tel: 098-25166, fax: 25090, www.theolderailwayhotel.com. Exceptionally comfortable, in the centre of town, building dates from 1780. €€

Wexford

White's Hotel, George Street, tel: 053-22311, fax: 45000, www.whiteshotel.ie. Partly modern, partly old, comfortable town hotel. €€
Clonard House, Clonard Great (4km/ 2 miles west of Wexford), tel/fax: 053-43141,www.clonardhouse.com. Pretty 18th-century farmhouse with B&B. €

YOUTH HOSTELS

The Irish Youth Hostel Association – An Oige, 61 Mountjoy Street, Dublin 7, tel: 01-830 4555, fax: 830 5808, www.irelandyha.org – runs around 37 establishments across the Republic.

Northern Ireland's equivalent is the Youth Hostel Association of Northern Ireland, or YHANI, 22 Donegal Road, Belfast BT12 5JN, tel: 028-9032 4733, www.hini.org.uk.

There are also several independent organisations right across Ireland which have now formed the Independent Holiday Hostels of Ireland, or IHH, 21 Store Street, Dublin 1, tel: 01-836 4700, fax: 836 4710, www.hostels-ireland.com. These are preferred by many to the rather stricter 'official' establishments.

*Seafood at Sweeney's
Oughterard House*

INDEX